T Gospel with a *Twist* and more…

Creative Inspiration		Thought-Provoking
Motivating	Humorous	Encouraging
Convicting		Healing
Poetic Verse		Love and Romance

I Bet You Never Heard It Like This!

Shirley Collins

ISBN 978-1-0980-9327-3 (paperback)
ISBN 978-1-0980-9329-7 (hardcover)
ISBN 978-1-0980-9328-0 (digital)

Christian Faith Publishing
832 Park Avenue
Meadville, PA 16335
www.christianfaithpublishing.com

Printed in the United States of America

From the depths of my heart, I dedicate this book to my daughter, Kennedy, the apple of my eye; my eleven-year-old grandson, Keshawn, and his mom, Jalisa; my extended family, Jessica and her twins, eight-year-old Jace and Jailani; Marcus, a young co-worker, who captured my heart with his brilliant talents, is now considered as family; and my honorary son, Matthew (from age seventeen to now age thirty). He loves, cherishes, and treats me like I am his very own...*loan after loan!* With the bond of a mother's love, I always comply.

A special dedication goes to my *entire* enormous family, who gives "honor and respect" to my position as the "matriarch" of the family tree although I am not the oldest. (There are ten older nieces and nephews.)

The overflow of love and support from each "sibling's branch" magnifies anew and unconditionally as the years go by.

Sonny Boy

Gertha

Lou

Vel

Jess

Bob

Harvey

Joe C.

Thanks. I love you all!

To the Reader

I hope you enjoy the array of selections as much as I have had composing them. Each piece has its own story. As I occasionally read them over and over again, it excites joy and amusement to laugh, cry, sing, praise the Lord, or whatever reactions the setting brings forth. I envision those similar effects will take place as the messages penetrate your hearts and minds.

As a reminder, life experiences will teach you many things as you mature from adolescence to adulthood. Every emotion in your being will be put to the test, some more than others. There may be joy and sorrow, love and happiness, heartache and pain, strengths and weaknesses, and triumphs and failures.

Do not be dismayed; you are not alone. Everyone will have his or her own challenges to bear. What may appear to be a catastrophe will serve as the stimulant to mold you to become stronger and wiser. Such times or incidents teach principles that carry profound moral influence and lay the foundation for a lasting impact on the progression of your life. What better way "to learn a lesson," than "to experience the lesson."

Do not allow disappointments to stunt your spiritual growth. Whether good or bad, the Bible teaches us that "*all things" work together for the good for those who love God*" (Romans 8:28 CSB).

Tip:

Words of Wisdom: *"When in doubt, leave it out!"*
This is a rewarding and reliable word of advice.
It's the perfect solution when making difficult decisions.
It takes the *worry* out of the problem.
It eliminates the fear of consequences.
It acts as a measure of protection.
It persuades the *gut feeling* to respond appropriately when a situation doesn't look right.

Connect online at www.atthemercyseat.com.

Acknowledgments

Throughout the years, there have been many people whose words of encouragement and acts of kindness helped to make me who I am and where I am at the present. I owe thanks and give faces to this collage of admirers, supporters, and well-wishers. *As a collage has no order of placement*, nor are the acknowledgments listed in order of my appreciation.

First of these I want to acknowledge is the minister of music, Chester D. T. Baldwin (Riceville Mount Olive Baptist Church, Houston, Texas). Chester was enthusiastically encouraging with the mention of my writings at "first sight." His believing in me ignited an extra ounce of courage to move forward. More than just a booster, he challenged my sincerity and accountability by giving me a timeline to the finish line. Thanks, Chester! This is only phase I.

I give high regards to my favorite high school English teacher and role model, Mr. Marrage Facen. His humorous teaching style made a great impact on my ability to grasp and internalize information as it is taught. There was never a dull moment in his class, even during the time when we had to produce an impromptu theme (short essay) by the end of class "every day." However, it helped to develop my thinking skills, which only strengthened my natural creativity. Thanks, Mr. Facen, for being such an inspiration to my life and teaching career.

I pay homage to the memory of Rev. Willie Flix, one of my greatest supporters, who just could not wait for this book. He would often nod and sleep throughout the entire church service. However, my presentations captured his undivided attention. He would lean forward and park a grin on his face for a delightful treat as he eagerly awaited the climax of the story. Rest in peace, Rev.! You can tuck my book away under your soft pillow of clouds.

Rev. Harvey Bowden, I appreciate the continuous accolades and words of encouragement throughout the years as well. Now "the wait is over." I am sure this book will *inspire a message for at least one sermon.*

I owe special thanks to Constance Darby for her sincere and uplifting message of appreciation at a time when I needed it the most. I remember the little redhead girl with a big thick-braided ponytail cheerfully marching and singing in step. Now it has come full circle. She is all grown up as a dynamic Christian Motivational Speaker, Praising the Lord. Thanks again, Constance, and may the grace of God continue to bless and take you to higher heights.

I am indeed thankful for Michelle Marks Turner, one of my co-matrons with the church drill team. She always had faith in me and trusted my ability to produce new material in a crunch. When other churches would inquire about where we purchased our material, Michelle would proudly strut and say, "This is exclusively for our team and not available for sale." On one occasion, I had botched up a song "royally" according to my standards. But Michelle was over the moon in love with it and insisted that I not change a thing. Well, it has been over fifteen years and who could have imagined in 2020, the title of the song, *Trump*, would bear such a dissimilarity with another well-known person named "Trump." Finally, I got the opportunity to make changes. With all due respect to the biblical story it reflects (David and Goliath), and for clarity, the new name for this song is "God Is the Highest Trump!" Thanks, Michelle, I know I have your usual consent of approval.

In loving memory of Nell Deloris Rambo. I owe the utmost gratitude for her unwavering love and the influence she had on my life from early childhood. She never failed to remind me that, out of all of my accomplishments, she was most proud of the *fine* adult I grew up to be. I remember in first grade wanting to be a teacher like her because she was extra nice and stood tall and beautiful in her tight skirt with high heel shoes. She was my brother's sixth-grade teacher at the time, but I would spend countless sleepovers at her house.

Throughout the years until her demise (April, 2017), she often told the story of when she took me on an exciting trip to Las Vegas when I was seven years old. She was very impressed by my spunky demeanor and the ability to have spontaneous conversations with total strangers. That trip was an unforgettable and heartwarming experience for both of us; we were bonded for life. Her son, Eddie, was only a year older but he preferred to stay home to be spoiled by the grandparents. I will always cherish the fond memories of summers on the farm and how she doted over me for being the daughter she never had. Now, Eddie and I will continue to occasionally ride by the property to keep the memories alive! Our dearest *Mama Nell*, may you rest in heaven's glory and eternal love.

I have to mention my nephew/brother Nathan Jackson. We grew up together and we're always fighting because he will "snap" in an instant when he can't win the argument. "*Furthermore*," he loves to s-t-r-e-t-c-h the truth. However, win or lose, we never fail to have each other's back. He's always there to support whatever I do. Thank you, Nate!

Lastly, three years ago in 2017, I joined Steve Harvey's *Jump with Steve Success Club*, because I needed ongoing motivation and supervision. The club provided a step-by-step plan to coach and guide you along the way until your goal was accomplished. This was exactly what I was looking for; therefore, I signed up for the challenge.

Immediately afterward, *all dams broke lose in my life*. "My *jump*" landed me in a world equivalent to a pool of quicksand! I was stuck in multiple circumstances that kept me from making progress toward my goal. I bought Steve's book, *Jump*, but I never had the chance to read it. I received daily planning tools through email, but I couldn't keep up with the tasks. The more I tried to prioritize and declutter the situation, the deeper I sank! After a week or two, I was too *stressed* and *stretched* to continue because things were worse than ever. I suffered back-to-back calamities that were severe and unforeseen! I was forced to hit the "pause" button.

To make a long story short, I had failed to meet the deadlines for 2018 and then again for 2019. Therefore, the new time limit was set for February 2020. I knew this target date was really impractical, with all the typing, editing, and research that still needed to be done; however, I wanted to move full speed ahead with no room to *procrastinate.*

Then out of nowhere, the Lord came to my rescue through the pandemic shutdown! Everything came to a halt! I was legally given a pass to say "no" to everybody and everything that were a hindrance in my efforts to move forward in a timely manner. At last, the chaos that had me bound was instantly lifted! Now, I had a peaceful environment to clear my mind and let the thoughts flow. I took full advantage of my newly found "free days." Every chain that held me back was broken. What a joyous feeling to be able to see light at the end of the tunnel!

It's been three years in the making, but as of September 2020, I finally finished the book! *The Jump Challenge* kept me grounded to "my commitment" to never give up!

"My faith" provided an avenue in disguise to have all the "quiet time" I needed. I give all praises to God for preparing me to utilize such precious and valuable moments, which were an overall defining period within itself. I also learned to appreciate the simple things in life. I feel like the "shutdown" was a "blessing with my name on it!"

Thank you, Lord, for putting me on the right path and guiding me through until the end.

Contents

My Story 15
Introduction 27

Poems and Inspirational Readings
    The High Cost of Low Living 31
    I Was Conned! 35
    God Doesn't Have to Use You and Me 40
    It's a "King" Thing 42
    Get "Self" Out of the Way 47
    A Letter to God 49
    God Has Done Great Things… Thus, He Has
    Done Great Things for Me 52
    Thanks for Your Word 55
    The Writing on the Wall 57
    Order My Steps in Your Word to Follow the
    Yellow Brick Road 60
    Daniel in the Lion's Den 65
    The Mighty Fire 67
    Women's Liberation 69
    I Don't Want Rocks Crying Out for Me 73
    The Master Has Done Great Things 75
    The Magical Three (3) 78
    Clichés That Lead Us Astray 79
    The DeGreprobate State(s) 83
    Sleep Tight 89

Holidays and Special Occasions
    'Twas the Day before Christmas 93
    Dad: A Father's Day Salute 96

Mother, You're Every Woman: A Mothers' Day Salute.......98
A Prayer of Blessings on "Fathers' Day"...........................100
One Little Thing..103

People, Special Request, and Special Occasions
Rev. Joe Dean Johnson..107
Joe D. 108
Excerpts and Words of Wisdom 111
The Makings of You: Annotation....................................117
The Makings of You..118
Mr. Short Stuff: Annotation..120
Mr. Short Stuff...121
The Big "Five-O": Annotation 124
The Big "Five-O" 125
It's Your Twenty-Fifth Anniversary! (Annotation) 127
It's Your Twenty-Fifth Anniversary! 128
More than a Woman to Me (Annotation) 130
More than a Woman to Me...131
The Greatest Champ Annotation....................................133
The Greatest ChampPoem Annotation 135
The Greatest Champ..137

Others
A Few Moments with You..141
Life Is a Rainbow without You 142
The Heart..144
My Clothes Won't Cooperate: Annotation 145
My Clothes Won't Cooperate 146

Appendix A: Note of Thanks..151
Appendix B: "Clearly Outstanding" Performance
    Assessment Record 153
Appendix C: Biblical Reference 155
The High Cost of Low Living..155
God Doesn't Have to Use You and Me............................160
It's a "King" Thing 165

God Has Done Great Things… Thus, He Has
Done Great Things for Me...169
The Writing on the Wall...170
Daniel in the Lion's Den 173
The Mighty Fire..176
I Don't Want Rocks Crying Out for Me..........................178
The Magical Three (3) 182
The Master Has Done Great Things 185
The DeGreprobate State(s) 187

One Wish...190

My Story

Everybody has a story, and to know me, you must know my "story." Here are a few pages from chapters in my life on a journey to "teach" or whatever it was destined to be, as long as it came with a "degree." As I share "my story" with you, remember that each "act" always ends the same: *Giving up is not an option.*

I came from humble beginnings, with a myriad of hardships and adversities while carving my way from small-town high hopes to making big-city dreams come true. I attended Adams Elementary School in rural Lake Providence, Louisiana (East Carroll Parish). My family moved to town when I was in the third grade, but I continued to attend school in the country throughout my elementary years. I rode to school with the teachers because several of them lived on my street. I was a fast learner, very energetic, well mannered, and highly respectful; therefore, the staff was delighted to keep me on board.

There was a change of venue for my middle school years. I became lonely because the only friends I had in town were the Kleinpeter family, who lived across the street, directly in front of our house (they would later in life become my extended family). There was Annie Elizabeth, a year older, and Anita, two years younger. The age difference was okay; however, they had other friends while I had only them. I longed for my classmates who lived miles away in the country.

As a remedy for that situation, in sixth grade, I convinced my parents to allow me to transfer to the school in town, Carroll Elementary. I had no problems making new friends or fitting in because of my cheerful, outgoing personality. However, the "real" reason I wanted to transfer was because the junior high classes (seventh and eighth grades) were on the campus of G. W. Griffin High School, and I wanted to be "in the mix" with the high school students and "all the happenings." I did not want to wait until seventh grade. I wanted to go as "pre-established with friends" as opposed to arriving "green on the scene." My mother was *very* strict. If she had known what my true motives were, the answer would have been a big fat *no*! And do not ask anymore!

School life was exciting. I made good grades, I got along well with my peers, and I shared a mutual relationship with my teachers of admiration and respect. I learned at an early age to practice my mother's most profound rule—obedience, good manners, and respect for "all" adults, not just teachers. She would always say, "Good manners will take you further than high marks." Without her saying a word, it was understood that "talking back to the teacher" was a "death sentence" in our household.

I attended G. W. Griffin High School from seventh through tenth grades until the schools were integrated. As part of the Civil Rights Movement, students were encouraged to enroll in the town's all-white school, Lake Providence High. I accepted the call. Attending the "White" school was pure misery! The staff and students made life and the learning environment almost intolerable. Black students had to endure name-calling, objects thrown, pranks, insensitive comments, you name it. During lunch, if one Black student sat at the opposite end of a table full of White students, then every student at the table would get up and move, leaving the Black student to sit alone. The same scenario occurred on bleachers in the gym, on the benches in the courtyard, in an assembly in the auditorium, or wherever we would congregate on campus. The staff condoned their behavior because nothing was done to prevent it or discouraged it.

I was always an A/B honor roll student each grading period. My White speech teacher made it her mission to blemish my report card by making it impossible to get a grade higher than a C. Her opinionated assessment would always minimize my test grades. I took the class only to advance my natural-born creativity skills because I have always had a passion for poetry and imaginative writing. I did not need the credits to graduate; therefore, I decided to drop the class, only to be denied by the assistant principal. He stated that a grade of C was good enough for "you people," which only confirmed that his view of Blacks included mediocrity and inferiority. His remarks only fueled my ambitions to get a college education!

To my knowledge, Lake Providence High did not offer career day, career counseling, or college tours. (At least, the Black students were not aware.) It was left up to the students to seek this information on their own. I was blessed and fortunate to have an older friend, Irene Layton (my big sister), who had high expectations for me. She took me under her wing in middle school and was my confidant who cared for me with genuine love and sisterly advice throughout the following years. She was a shoulder to lean on whom I could share personal issues without judgment. Earlier in my high school sophomore year, she took the responsibility to introduce me to college life for a week stay at Grambling State University, where she attended summer school. I was in awe…my first time to set foot on a college campus.

I was twice blessed when I had the opportunity to go on a field trip to Southern University with the students from the Black school, G. W. Griffin High in my junior year. The campus at Southern University was so beautiful and twice the size of Grambling. The beige-colored brick buildings only made them seem brighter and taller. The designs of the Triangle Dormitories were unique and impressive. But the icing on the cake was The Villa Apartments, with a pool out front and no curfew! *Wow!* However, only juniors, seniors, and married students could live there. It would take me another three to four years to even meet the qualifications. But that did not matter, with the sky being the limit, it only gave me the incentive "to reach for another star"! We finished the trip with a movie, *To Sir with Love*, starring Sidney Poitier and lunch at Piccadilly Cafeteria.

Visiting Southern University was a memorable experience of a lifetime for a small-town girl like me with high hopes of seeing an elusive dream of going to college finally coming into view. Yes, it was there on a beautifully landscaped campus with the banks of the mighty Mississippi River backdrop in Baton Rouge, LA, that I set my *mind, heart,* and *soul* to attend Southern University.

I was all hyped up for going to college with no means of getting there. I literally did not have a clue where to begin. Remember, Lake Providence High did not provide any college information. At the time, I had no guidance on how to apply for a state loan, had never heard of work study programs, and surely didn't know about grants that didn't require repayment. Who would not want to take full advantage of such opportunities that are *free*? Nevertheless, I was on my own with no help, and I had to come up with a plan because *"giving up" was not an option.*

In the early '70s, tuition fees were only $500 per semester. My plan was to work every summer and earn a $1,000 to pay tuition for the upcoming year. Quite simple and doable…so I thought. I had a strong determination and good work ethic—skills that prepared me for the challenge. During the summer, I worked at the Head Start program for the elementary school and during the holidays as a salesclerk at the town's five and dime store (which was called the ten-cent store for short).

I had also been a regular babysitter for several teachers, where I learned time management, responsibility, and accountability, which are all essential aspects of a job. There was one couple with whom I shared a special bond, Joel and Geraldine Hawkins. They both were my teachers, but as fate would have it, Mrs. Hawkins was my rock and support at the "White" school. (She was one of the few Black teachers who also transferred to Lake Providence High.) Later in my college life, she would be the instrument that saved me and changed the course of my life.

After high school graduation in May, I put my plan in motion and went to live with my brother's family in Houston, Texas, for the summer. At first, I did not find a job immediately as planned. Around the end of June, almost two months later, I accepted a job as a bill collector, but it paid only minimum wage of $1.30 an hour which grossed about $52.00 weekly. Minus taxes, bus fare, and lunch, my net earnings were about $30.00 each week. Regardless, I continued working while applying for other jobs.

F inally, it was September. The fall semester rolled around, and I did not have the finances to enroll at Southern. I never knew what being poor felt like until that moment. This made me realize that no matter how well life is going, you may be "one day" from becoming the less fortunate. My heart ached as the ship that I should have been aboard sailed without me. I met all the qualifications...acceptance letter in hand, bags packed, yet I was left behind. My body became emotionally weak and limp from the sadness in my heart. After a few days of sobbing, I cut the "pity party" short. Again, *giving in to a minimum wage job was definitely not an option!* I said, "Well, Lord, it's just You and me. Let's go!"

I had to go to plan B. Oh yes, I always make a plan B along with plan A. I decided to seek help. I really did not want to go there, but desperate situations call for desperate actions. I did not want to stay out of school for a whole year when I could always make up lost time during the summer, so I went back home and expressed my desires to my dad.

Without hesitation, he mortgaged our home to borrow the $500 tuition fee for me to start school in January, the spring semester. I promised I would pay it back. He proudly smiled and said, "When you get your degree, that will be payment enough." I could stop here and say, "The rest is history," but God was not through with me yet.

School was out in May, so I went back to plan A. Only this time, I went to Las Vegas, Nevada. I landed a job immediately through the Union as a maid at one of the leading hotels on the Las Vegas Strip. Now, I had the opportunity to work a full three months and pay cash for the next school year. The job paid $15.00 a day, which was good in the early '70s. Instantly, I had an encouraging flashback on how my mom, who managed the finances on a moderate income, was a genius at "making ends meet." Although we lived comfortably and never went lacking for the necessities of life, it was her budgeting tactics that made all the difference. Our household was a true example of how *God does not count dollars*; rather, *He makes dollars count!* Since this hotel job was promising, I was mindful to apply her same principles and to expect the same favorable outcome.

After working only one week at the hotel, I was fired, with no explanation. I could not understand it! I was only nineteen years old with no hotel experience, but I was very enthusiastic about my job and worked the hardest to prove myself. The other maids were moved by my story to go to college, enough to teach me the "ropes" and help when needed, in cleaning the twelve rooms assigned per day. I had not told anyone about my dismissal, but they were all asking why I got fired. Little did I know that the "pink slip" waving in my hand meant "terminated."

My sister told me not to worry because the hotels needed maids every day. "Just go back to the Union," she said, "and put your name on the list and wait for them to call you up for another assignment." I had no time to lose, so the very next morning, I was there when the doors opened. Sure enough, my name was called for a new assignment. Ironically, it was the same position at the same hotel I had just been fired from the day before. When I reported for duty, the supervisor had "egg on her face" when she looked up and saw that my replacement was "me!" As she grudgingly gave me my room assignments, her comments were, "You're too high-minded. I didn't go to college, and I'm your boss." The other maids were excited to see me back and noted that the supervisor was just jealous, so they vowed to help with my rooms so I could keep my job to pay those tuition fees. They even whispered how proud they were of me to stand up to her. They assumed I had reported her for firing me without a valid cause. However, I did not take the credit for doing anything. "I just showed up," but "God showed out!"

I worked an extra week or two in September just to get double time for working on Labor Day. I had worked three full months—June, July, and August. I saved my entire paycheck. I did not spend a dime, not even for a popsicle from the ice cream truck. When I was asked to buy anything, my firm response was, "*No, I got to pay my tuition!*" For years, I was teased yet applauded by that statement. My sister's contribution was to allow me to live with her for the summer "free of charge." I took full advantage of the offer.

I went to Vegas on a Greyhound bus, but I came back home on Delta Airlines. This was my first time flying. I had so many mixed emotions with each trying to outweigh the other…nervous, excited, overjoyed, grateful, but humble most of all. My mission was accomplished. I matured a lot that summer…not in age but in my faith and trust in God. With all the love and support I had from teachers and loved ones, nobody—not one of them—thought to ask or advise me concerning financial assistance or other means of getting into college. I thought, *They all failed me.* Then, as I continued gazing through the window into the wild blue yonder, reflecting on my "tuition journey," I suddenly realized that God had set me up with road blocks, setbacks, and disappointments so that I could watch Him bring me through. Moreover, He prepared my heart and mind to *know* it was *Him.*

God has a great sense of humor, and He is full of surprises. When I arrived back home, I only had one day to regroup before going back to school. I was already excited about my summer earnings and anxious to leave, but to add to the hype and jubilation, there was a letter waiting for me from the government. It stated that my recent student loan application for financial aid had been approved for the remaining three years, and my check was waiting in the Financial Aid Office on campus. Oh, Happy Day! My parents celebrated in joy to see a burden lifted. It was their relief also because they equally shared the depth of my struggles as well as the uncertainty of how the next finances would come.

The student loan did not cover summer school. Again, God had already made provisions. Like my mother, He knew I was tight with money and had good management skills to save. Therefore, the money I earned that particular summer would pay for the next year's summer classes for me to catch up. The debt was paid forward. Now, I could focus solely on my education.

On my "college degree journey," God had many blessing up His sleeve. Coming up to my senior year, I had finally moved to the Villa Apartments...two bedrooms with two students in each room. All four of us got a job working in the school's cafeteria on the serving line. A new wing of the building was opened for athletes only. Professors and other staff could dine there as well. As a punishment for our chattering too much with students coming through the line, the supervisor reassigned me and my friends to the athlete's wing. I put on a sad face and acted disappointed so she would not change her mind. All along I was thinking, "To God be the glory! I have died and gone to heaven! Go ahead, Ms. Supervisor, throw me into the 'briar patch,' because this is exactly where I want to be." What was so ironic was that many of the athletes were our hang-out and partying buddies, so we were overjoyed to serve them. We gave them and the professors the *royal* treatment (all-you-can-eat and take).

I had taken a full load (eighteen to twenty-one hours) or as many hours possible for two semesters to make up the hours for the semester I had missed. However, strategizing and planning ahead, I still needed to take four classes (twelve hours) in summer school, but *six hours was the maximum allowed*, and there were no other times available for me to meet my goal and finish in three and a half years. I was faced with a tough dilemma. The fall semester was football season and a heavy class schedule during this time would have been too stressful to manage. Regardless, that was the only alternative. It was *a must* to complete all hours that were needed to graduate and have those extra classes behind me. I needed a clear mind to focus and prepare for the final challenge—student teaching. The upcoming spring semester leading to graduation was totally reserved for student teaching only.

To apply for summer school, the forms stating the classes and hours, required the dean's approval. I was an education major and the Dean of Education, whom signature I needed, was one of the professors who had regularly utilized the new dining facility on campus where I worked. When I went to his office, I was nervous yet prayerful to present such an enormous request of twelve hours, however, *my back was against the wall* and I had to go for it. The secretary said she was instructed to turn anyone away who listed more than six hours. At first, I was polite and asked to talk to the dean myself, but he refused to see me. I had to think fast because I knew that he probably did not know my name; that is why I wanted a chance for him to see my face. Then as I attempted to leave, the secretary turned her back while looking through the files, so I quickly poked my head in his door and said, "Good afternoon, Dean." He stood up and greeted me with a warm smile and handshake. He remembered my kind and friendly personality from the athlete's dining hall and how well we served the staff that came through the line. Through occasional small talk, as we cleaned the tables, my roommates and I would boast about becoming seniors and finally seeing graduation in sight. Moreover, I had personally mentioned to him how I'd had a shaky beginning. Therefore, he was familiar with my situation. When he learned that I was the one who was seeking approval for twelve hours, he admitted that my request was a bit much to ask. Nevertheless, he admired my eager persistence to achieve my goals and was more impressed with the tenacity of my determination under pressure. With his blessings for a successful future, the dean kindly signed the form.

Some say I have the "gift of gab," but I say, it is "favor" from the Lord. God put me in the *right place* to see the *right face* and to receive *an act of grace*. He made sure I was on the *right "serving line"* at the *right time to get a crucial form signed*. When you do your part and "show up," "God will do the rest!"

My faith and determination had paid off. I went on to graduate in May within three and a half years with a Bachelor of Science degree in business education with a minor in office administration. I moved to Houston in 1975 and accepted the first job in my field of business as an accounts receivables analyst with a major oil company. Although I enjoyed the executive glamour of the corporate setting, the job was not fulfilling. After working there for six years, I left the company and started substitute teaching while attending Texas Southern University to attain certifications in other teaching areas to broaden my qualifications for employment. Amid finding the right job, I never neglected my faith. I also had to find the right church; therefore, I united with the Riceville Mount Olive Baptist Church in Houston, Texas, in 1976 under the leadership of Pastor Joe D. Johnson.

I visited churches all over Houston, but Riceville was the perfect match for my spirit. Unlike some of the other big fancy churches with a huge congregation, Riceville sat on a graveled road, off the beaten path. The choir did not have a musician, and the pastor often stuttered in his message delivery, but he appeared to be humble and loved the Lord. Nevertheless, I felt right at home because the church welcomed me with loving arms and appreciation for what I had to offer. I joined that choir. And when the pastor started walking through those scriptures, the stuttering walked away. The Riceville Church family, as a whole, has been a blessing to me and my spiritual growth. Most importantly, it has given me a platform through the church Drill Team *to teach* Bible stories to the youth through songs, jingles, and live performances.

Thus, the church gave me support, encouragement, and an avenue to give uplifting, spiritual presentations throughout the years.

I have always had a passion for teaching and working with the youth. My strongest desires were to be able to use my knowledge and creativity to train and direct young minds to explore and develop the talents within themselves—to motivate and help build self-confidence to overcome barriers and feel free to function among their peers and society. Most of these aspects of a teacher do not come from a textbook or other technology equipment but from love, dedication, and compassion from the heart. This was the main ingredient I had to offer—the traits of a natural-born teacher. I firmly believe, as I often quote my pastor, "Every child has something to win with!"

I ended up earning my Texas Teacher Certification from the University of Houston. In 1987, I started my teaching career with the Houston Independent School District as a full-time business education teacher. Each academic year, I taught four to five subjects as assigned, which included typing, accounting, recordkeeping, business management, computer, etc. Having more than three preparations was stressful and beyond the call of duty. However, I persevered and demonstrated how I could become one of the best of the best teachers in the profession. I have an ongoing challenge to compete with *myself to implement new ideas and strategies* for the sake of my students and their parents who entrust their children in my care.

During this same time, I also taught evening classes at The Houston Community College Night High School for five years. One summer I was selected to be a part of the curriculum writing team to create action-oriented activities for the district's latest adopted accounting textbook. As much as I loved this challenge and seeing my original innovative ideas in print, I had to let it go because of a conflict between the two day/night teaching jobs and my "sanity." I had no summer break and worked year-round except the holidays.

Once again, my hard work had paid off and come full circle. It was over fifteen years in the making. Not only did I get the teaching position I desired but also had a principal who recognized and applauded great talent. My principal, whose last name was also "Collins," was impressed and pleased how I had taken her constructive criticism to heart from an earlier evaluation. *At my first year-end assessment conference*, she stated, "You've made every improvement I've asked you to do and more; your overall performance has earned my confidence that you will continue to be a great teacher. Therefore, I proudly give you the highest rating possible, "Clearly Outstanding!"

The bar was set high, and by the grace of God, I maintained the same high standards throughout my entire teaching career of twenty-six years. "Striving for perfection" can be overwhelming sometimes, yet it is exciting and satisfying because I cannot rest until I have given it my best!

My "story" of *rewards* and *testimonies* is merely a "life lesson" taught by God, the Master Teacher: *When giving up is not an option!*

Trust in the LORD with all your heart, and lean not unto your own understanding. In all your ways acknowledge him, and he shall direct your paths. (Prov. 3: 5–6 NKJV).

Introduction

Need an uplifting word from God, a test for your faith, or simply a reconnection with family, loved ones, reality, or even yourself? Proverbs 17:22 states that a merry heart (laughter) does good, like a medicine, and who doesn't occasionally need a good belly laugh? This volume of memorable entries is the answer to these and other questions and hopefully will positively transform your thoughts, your spirit, and possibly your view of your world.

Spanning over thirty-five years, this wide-range collection of creative inspiration focuses on almost every genre, including fiction, nonfiction, jingles, poetic verse, drama, and storytelling. Often thought-provoking but also humorous and entertaining, this volume contains something for every individual and circumstance. Many entries relate not only to present situations and calamities but also to past events. From touching ministers to reaching adolescents, the writings are designed to encourage, inform, and motivate, as well as foster a desire to spend more time reading and studying God's Word.

Categories include, but are not limited to, biblical references, love and romance, and holidays and special occasions—all designed to give hope, to make amends, to bring joy and laughter, to convict, and ultimately, to give peace of mind. It is hoped that time after time readers will be left with the conviction that heaven is right here on earth, as stated in the Lord's Prayer ("Thy kingdom come, thy will be done on earth, as it is in heaven"), and will believe that there is a reward in this life for serving the Lord and making Him your choice.

Poems and Inspirational Readings

The High Cost of Low Living

There's nothing under the sun
That hasn't been unturned.
What man is doing today
Has already been done.

Although his wisdom and knowledge
May have produced a more perfected scheme,
Man can't devise anything in the sight of God
That He hasn't already seen.

King David had a child with Bathsheba.
From her husband, he had this to conceal.
So David concocted his "master plan"—
To make sure her husband would be killed.

This "adultery and murder combo"
Was "the last straw" of his dirty dealings.
God took the child's life and made David pay
The high cost of low living.

Like David, men are still the same
I do declare!
Misleading a woman here, sleeping over there,
With a wife and baby elsewhere.

Their pockets are always empty,
And paycheck already spent,

Trying to keep up more than one household,
Leaving them worth less than two *cents*.

The pressure it brings is so killing,
But to let one of them go, they're unwilling.
Until they decide, just wipe those "lying" eyes
That's the price you have to pay for low living.

As one can see, man's conduct
Is such a disgrace, and *rancid* stained.
But if we look a little further, we'll also see
That women's actions are *smeared* quite the same.

"The Fall of Jezebel" sounds like
The destruction of a city.
Actually, it was the crashing of a seductress woman,
Whom no one cared to take pity.

She could throw her charm on a man
And turn him around and about.
But I wonder what happened to her charm that day
When through a window, she came tumbling out!

"Miniskirts" and "splits" helped society to pave the way.
All a woman needs to do is "the *walking*,"
Her *accentuating* dress will do "the *talking*."
And men will become easy, vulnerable, prey.

Many of today's women
Have taken on the Jezebel trait.
Be careful, ladies, with just one little "slip,"
You can also take on her fate.

You swindle, you connive, you even blink your eyes,
And call the shots for all do's and don'ts.

Instead of being ashamed, you continue to play the game
Of "using what you got to get what you want."

Credit can be given to Delilah,
For playing this game the best,
Because she "used what she had" on Samson
And got what she needed to get.

Samson was warned against the Philistine women
Still, having Delilah was a must!
In the end, he lost it all,
For the price of a "*bad haircut.*"

The power under his cap
Was no match
For the power in her lap!

Like a bird,
Samson began to sing,
Revealing the "secret in details," and
E-v-e-r-y other t-h-i-n-g!

His strength, respect, and even his sight
Were all gone instantly.
That's the *cost* you can expect,
When sleeping with the enemy.

Ladies, clean up your act now,
Any day could be the end of the line.
You never know how close you are,
Even Jezebel ran out of time.

She didn't get the chance to turn her life around,
To experience God's grace and healing.
"Push" came to "shove" which made her pay
The high cost of low living.

However, not everyone who suffers from sin
Can be put in the same "lowlife" boat
As there's one man who *never* sinned,
Yet he had to pay the highest note.

Jesus is this peculiar fellow,
Whom to this world, He did not bend.
Upon His shoulders, He bore the cross,
For the redemption of "our" sins.

Although the bloody scene at Calvary was chilling,
Until the last breath, Jesus remained forgiving.
Submissively, He died on the cross,
And paid The *Highest Cost of All*—
To save the "whole world" from *low living*.

I Was Conned!

Other than normal Christian beliefs, people come to Christ for various reasons—a near-death experience, loss of a loved one, alcohol or drug addiction, and so on. For me, my circumstances were totally different; I was conned!

First, I was CONfronted by the Ten Commandments. They kept haunting me and ringing in my ear with question after question. Each commandment demanded an answer:

I.   Is the "*I Am" God your "only" God* or is He just #1 on your list?

II. What *idol(s)* do you worship *in the place of God*? Is it a statue of a certain image as that of the golden calf, a cult leader like Jim Jones, or your earthly possessions?

III. Do you *take the name of the Lord in vain* for worldly benefits or other personal gain?

IV. Do you reference the *Sabbath Day* as a *holy* day of worship? Or do you count it as an uncalculated thought of "come what may," such as *a great day* for leisure activities, to catch up on your sleep for the busy week ahead, to recuperate from *Saturday night,* or all of the above?

V.   Do you *honor your father and mother with respect* and adhere to their advice, or do you "think you know it all" and disregard their counsel?

VI.   Do you have a vengeful heart *to kill* in cold blood and cry self-defense as an only option to settle a dispute, or are you willing to find other law-abiding means of justice?

VII.   Would you *commit adultery* at any cost? Would you risk destroying the livelihood of your family and/or facing public humiliation by *succumbing to lust*?

VIII. Would you *steal and take things that don't belong to you* just because no one is watching, or are you trustworthy?

IX.   Do you *lie* and participate in spreading gossip against your neighbor, friends, and others, or do you stop a negative rumor in its tracks?

X.   Are you *envious and jealous of your neighbor's* fine car and Lakeside home, or are you grateful for how the Lord has blessed you?

Yes, I was conned! *Con*fronted by the Commandments of God.

My next con job came when I was CONvicted. Every time I promised and tried to do good, evil was always present and made it easier for me to do wrong. The things I vowed in my heart not to do were the very things I found myself doing. The things I wanted to do or should have done, I did not do. Then I realized, "I'm in the middle of a terrible battle between the members of my mind; there's a war going on and I'm on the "front line." I said to myself, "Oh wretched and miserable person am I to be in such a sorrowful predicament! I've been conned again—*con*victed and found guilty by my sins, thus falling short of the glory of God. If that wasn't bad enough, I was CONdemned to die, because the wages of sin is a death sentence.

Yes, I was double-conned that time! *Con*victed and *con*demned by my own self-indulgence!

Realizing that I was doomed and fighting a losing battle, I needed *help*, so I welcomed the next con job with open arms. This

36

time, I was CONvinced—*con*vinced that the only one who could save and deliver me from this body of death is Jesus Christ. Thanks be to God, Jesus Christ has rescued me and made me *"free" from the law of sin and death.*

I've been conned! *Con*vinced that even though I'm destined to die, I shall have everlasting life through Jesus Christ!

Immediately and unstoppable, I felt another con job approaching…CONfession.

As I parted my lips to speak, a loud outcry abruptly broke through from the "strings of my heart," declaring, *I believe!*

I believe in the Trinity: Father, Son, and the Holy Ghost.

I believe that Jesus Christ is the son of God, and He was conceived of a virgin by the Holy Spirit.

I believe He was baptized by John as an example for man to follow.

I believe He lived a sinless life but took on the sins of the world so that we might have a right to the Tree of Life.

I believe He died and was buried, but on the third day, He got up with all power in His hand.

I believe He broke the chains of death that had us bound.

I believe that He ascended to heaven and is seated at the right hand of the Throne of God.

But most of all, I believe He's coming back for *"me!"*

I was compelled to *con*fess these things to the whole world because *I believe* that Jesus Christ is the only name in heaven or earth that a man can call on and be saved! Again, I was conned!

After confessing, I thought I was home free, but the conning didn't stop there. Somehow, I "looked" vulnerable. "I had *a con-attraction*," which led to "*a chain of con-reactions*." After reading, hearing, and seeing the word in action, I was double-conned once more!

This time, I was CONsumed by the power of the Holy Spirit and CONverted. I was born again! Old things became new. A transformation took place. It changed a deceitful, wicked, and stubborn heart *to a circumcised heart* with love and compassion. It brought rebirth through *baptism*, a *symbol on the outside* reflecting *the change on the inside* to trust and follow Christ. Although the rapture is yet to come, I became a new creature in this life.

I was conned—*con*sumed and *con*verted from sinner to a Christian/believer.

Now that I'd become a member of the Christian family, I had to be mindful of my whole way of living, thinking, learning how to approach ungodly people, handling business affairs, etc. This is when my next con job came on the scene.

I was CONducted by the Holy Scriptures with "explicit" instructions: (1) Be just in your dealings. "Dishonest gains always bring a curse on the soul." (2) Refrain from having a pretentious status. Don't boast. God hates a proud look. "He who thinks that he stands, take heed, least he falls." (3) Don't rejoice in someone's downfall. Pray for one another and be ready and willing to show brotherly love.

With these instructions, among others, I made a conscious decision to live by God's standards. Regardless of what is permissible in the world or what others may do, "*as for me and my house, we will serve the Lord.*"

I was conned—*con*ducted by the Holy Bible to be a "reader" and "doer" of God's Word. The Scriptures ironically "threw the book at me!"

God knows that Satan is too conning,
For me to fight him by myself.
So He sent a whole troop of "CON" men
To stand guard for around-the-clock help.

When I'm lonely and distressed
And no one seems to care,
He sends <u>Joy</u> to CONverse with me
To change the mood, *right then and there!*

If I attempt to make bad choices
Or risk ruining my reputation,
He sends <u>Willpower</u> to CONstrain me
To avoid a regrettable situation.

Sometimes this flesh is urged
To indulge in a sinful fling,
He sends <u>Commands</u> to CONtrol me,
From destroying a lifelong dream.

In case I "feel" high and mighty
Or have the "tendency" to gloat and brag,
He sends <u>Justice</u> to CONdense me
To no more than a filthy rag!

If I worry about this thorn in my side
Becoming unbearable to the touch,
He sends <u>Peace</u> to CONsole me,
That His Grace is sufficient enough!

But there are many times, I do good deeds,
Going exceedingly above and beyond,
He sends <u>Blessings</u> to CONfirm,
He's pleased at what I've done.

The most rewarding experiences I've had in life, second to none,
are the times when… I was conned!

God Doesn't Have to Use You and Me

If anyone chooses not to serve the Lord and follow His commands,
It doesn't hinder God, the least, from fulfilling his plans.

If man, beast, and everything that creeps should decide to keep still,
God will use the *elements of the universe* to do His will.

He used a *star* to show the world where baby Jesus would be.
He used Jordan's *muddy waters* to cure a rich man's disease.

To save a wedding from a flop, He turned *water* to *wine*.
He used His spit and *clay dirt* to give sight to the blind.

He used the *dew* on a fleece to encourage Gideon to fight.
He used the *sun* to stop Paul from destroying a Christian's life.

He used the *clouds* by day and *fire* by night
To lead the children of Israel with a guiding *light*.

He used the *shade* from a tree to cool Jonah's face.
He took that *shade tree* away to put Jonah in his place.

He used the *wind* to dry a path through the Roaring Red Sea.
He used that *sea* to swallow an army to set the captives free.

Sometimes destructive *weather* may leave us helpless in a daze. He sends His love through a *rainbow* to put a smile on our face.

Basically, if man fails to obey God's orders, just watch and behold. He will use *elements of the universe* to prove His control.

This earthly life is only a "dress rehearsal" to the ultimate "there-after" plans. A *blood-washed* ticket has been offered for man to have that chance.

If necessary, God will choose other methods, as you can plainly see. *He surely doesn't have to use you and me!*

It's a "King" Thing

Stories of Truth and Triumph

The Woman at the Well

What started out as an ordinary trip, made the town people think that the woman had flipped.

As the woman began to draw water,
This Jew asked her for a drink.
"Excuse me, I'm just a Samaritan," she replied.
"You've made a mistake, I think."

"You Jews don't give us the time of day
Or a second blink.
Now, you're asking me
To give you a drink?"

Jesus replied, "I understand your feelings
And what you might think,
But if you knew who I am,
You'd be asking me for a drink."

"The water I have is endless.
It renews and flows to the core.
Once you drink of me,
You will never thirst anymore."

"You say you have no husband,
And this, dear woman, is true.
You've had five others in the past,
But the one you're with now doesn't belong to you."

The woman dropped her vessel
And ran back to town
To tell the whole world
About the jewel she had found.

Come see a man who holds the future in his hands!

Everybody knew when they
Saw the look on her face
That something great had happened.
A drastic change had taken place.

The woman went to the well as a "deceiver;" miraculously, she came
back as a "believer."

This is the kind of joy it brings
When "King" Jesus steps on the scene!
        It's a "King" thing!

———

A Woman Caught Committing Adultery

The Pharisees confronted Jesus, saying,
"This woman was caught in the act and could not lie.
Now according to the Law of Moses,
To commit such a sin, she must surely die."

"You've been teaching us to abide by the law and do what's right.
Well, what do you have to say about this awful sight?"

Jesus casually ignored them as He wrote in the sand.
Still, the crowd demanded that He take a stand.

Jesus replied, "Since you insist on hearing my views,
Listen carefully, this goes for every one of you."
"Go ahead, kill her," He said, in a very calm tone.
"But let the one who has never sinned be the first to cast his stone."

Jesus ignored them once again and continued writing in the sand.

One by one, they all began
To drop their stones.
And when Jesus looked around,
They had shamefully gone home.

He asked the woman,
"Where did they go?
You mean to tell me,
Not one blow?"

"No, my Lord,"
She replied with a sigh.
"They couldn't condemn you," said Jesus.
"And neither do I."

"Let this be the end
Of the things you've done before.
Go, my child,
And sin no more."

"Conviction" and "deliverance" transpired at the same time.
This is what happens when King Jesus touches the mind.
It's a "King" thing!

———

Not only in biblical times, the United States have experienced a "*King*" *thing* in our lifetime.

Descendants of slavery were oppressed and depressed,
Living on shattered dreams.
But the Lord heard their cry and sent a leader,
His name was Martin Luther *King*.

Like Moses, he was a man of God who led his people well.
He took them to the "mountaintop," but his life ended there.
Fueled by King's struggles and sacrifice, the movement survived.
His milestone achievements, indeed, kept *hope* alive!

Coming "from the back of the bus" to "driving the bus,"
His legacy acclaimed a "peaceful, powerful, and productive" fight.
From "carrying an ID note" to "casting a vote,"
It was worth the challenges and obstacles to attain equal rights.

Martin Luther's last name just happened to be "King,"
But his works were the results from when the "*Almighty*" intervened.
It's a "King" thing!

––––––

The country is in such a state of agony, frustration, and pain!
Consequently, it will take "all the *King's* horses"
And "all the *King's* men"
To put it back together again.

First, the government took prayer out of school.
Then to spank your own child is a crime.
The rights of the parents are taken away.
There's a wonder why the children won't mind.

Massive shootings in schools have caused many *children* to die.
Yet permits for automatic weapons are at an all-time high.

45

Gangs and White supremacists are getting younger and younger.
Instead of making progress, we continue to go under.

Decades of sexual harassment
Are finally unmasked but well overdue.
Women united against their perpetrators,
With a movement saying "Me Too!"

Racism against minorities
Is back at the forefront in full swing.
It's far worse than the horrific "beat down"
Of a man named Rodney *King.*

Innocent Black men, in broad daylight,
Are being "shot down from the back"
While crooks and hate groups
Get a "pat and pardon" for their acts.

Justice for *all* is clearly not the same.
It's done "by status," "by color," and "by name."

Jesus left on record, a very simple plan:
If we seek His face
And turn from our wicked ways
He will surly heal the land!

The Almighty "King" is watching from His throne.
Martin Luther "King" completed his mission and passed on.
Rodney "King" left a message that's still going strong,
Crying out to the world, *"Can't we all just get along?"*

It's a "King" Thing!

Get "Self" Out of the Way

You never seem to have enough time
To give thanks to God each day.
You're so wrapped up in the cares of the world,
You fail to realize how He keeps making a way.

Are you in such a hurry
That you can't pause in silent prayer
To acknowledge the mere fact of being alive
Is evident how "considerably" God cares?

Are you too busy tweeting and messaging
That you don't have the time to bend a knee?
After all, it is God, not social media friends,
Whom you should be trying to please.

You're not that far gone in "failures"
That you're unworthy of a new start.
If you would make the effort, you'd find Jesus,
Just waiting to come into your heart.

It isn't pure luck that keeps your
Family secured, clothed, and fed,
But by the grace of God who protects us
And continuously watches overhead.

It isn't by chance to have good health, stability,
And conveniences of a comfortable home

But from the blessings of our loving God,
Who promises to never leave you alone.

It's not by coincidence that you've
Obtained wealth and a successful career,
But it is the will of our Lord
That we live happy and prosperous years.

Just think, if you receive all of these blessings
Without stopping to give thanks and praise,
Imagine an *overflowing cup*, if you put Christ first
And *get "self" out of the way*!

A Letter to God

Dear Heavenly Father,

Although this letter is marked "personal," it is not confidential because I want the whole world to know what I'm about to say, mainly, Satan.

Father, I've made some changes in my life and I've turned over a new leaf. You thought I was worth saving and gave me an opportunity to make a new start; therefore, I'd like to express my thankfulness through the channels of my heart.

Since the last time you heard from me, I'm a new person and this is what brought about the change: I discovered that the scripture stating, "The Holy Spirit will teach you all things and bring all things to your remembrance" is very true, especially the part "bring all things to your remembrance." As I reflect back over the years, I had a good Christian upbringing. I went to church, Sunday school, and even sang in the choir. I read the Bible regularly. There's one scripture that sticks with me like an overprotective parent. "Train up a child in the way he should go; even when he is old, he will not depart from it." It acts as a self-governing guide. It protects and convicts one to be mindful of the consequences of their actions and choices, whether good or bad…especially when you know or should have known better.

From early on as a teenager, I've always had the desire to be close to you, but when I left home, things seemed to take a different turn. I remember reading the scripture saying "first," seek the Kingdom of God and His righteousness, and everything else would be added unto you. That sounded like long-term advice, which would take years to achieve, so I consciously didn't adhere. I was too busy because "first," I had to finish college, then more college, and then it was my job and career. I just didn't have time for anything else, like going to church every Sunday and all the other religious duties that followed. I became consumed with the wonders of a young adult's lifestyle. I just wanted to explore life and have fun!

Although I had deep Christian values and I was taught to put all faith and trust in you, I still stumbled. Many times, I'd keep the faith, but only for a short while, and then give up to settle for whatever there was… never knowing that the victory would have been the very next day. I was often in a state of confusion because I had drifted away from you. This was not my idea of "having fun."

To be honest, Lord, I had a miserable life. You see, there were too many hard times, too many lonely nights, too many disappointments from friends and loved ones, and too many heartbreaks and heartaches. Lord, "too many" times like these made it "too hard" for me "to bear." They brought me so low until my knees took the place of my feet—I was on them the majority of the time, asking you Father, to please help me! Please take control of my life and make everything all right; please take charge of my soul and make me whole. Then, I let out a loud cry…a trembling, merciful cry from the depths of my heart. Suddenly, I felt a calmness come over me. "Your undying love overpowered my mind and pitied every groan." The very first time I humbled myself and asked your forgiveness, you came to my rescue and delivered me. You are the true on-time God that the elders sing about. Caught up in a spiritual bliss, I realized that you had been there all along, just waiting for me to acknowledge your presence.

I've had to learn the "hard way" that without You, there is "no other way." It took some years, but with maturity came wisdom, and fortunately, my life has been restored.

I love you, Lord! You put joy in my heart and gave me a personalized song to sing praises to your Holy Name. Now that I'm back with you, please don't let me go. If I tend to stray too far to the left or too far right, please redirect my course, but never ever let me go!

I know that "faith" is one of the main components of the Christian journey. The Bible says, all that is needed is a little faith; the size of a mustard seed and you'll be able to move mountains. Lord, I want to live up to the Christian name and be more Christlike, but I don't have the level *of faith that I desire, which is…"believing" without seeing, "knowing" without questioning, and "trusting" without doubting. Please increase my faith and double my determination to follow you.*

Consequently, this letter comes to you with "thanksgiving" and I'm sending it "special delivery," which describes how "extraordinary special" you are to me.

Lord, please send your Holy Spirit to teach me your ways:

To have "patience" like Sarah, who waited and gave birth to a child at an old age.

To be "loyal" and "obedient" like Noah, who built an ark for shelter from a flood when it had never rained.

To have the "trust" of Abraham, who was willing to sacrifice his only son's life on your behalf.

To be "pure in heart" like Enoch who went to heaven without dying.

To have the "faith" of Job, whom, after losing all ten of his children, all his possessions, and his entire body was covered with sores, he still praised your name.

Indeed, it would have been an honor to have my name written in the Bible as one of your faithful followers, and people could be inspired by reading about me throughout the world; unfortunately, that's not possible, because the Bible is already written. However, I still have a chance of getting into your book, Lord, and that's The Book of Life!

Father, I'm striving toward "seeing your face" on that great judgment day! When the heavenly roll book is opened, I pray that my name will have so many "stars and check marks" you will stretch out your arms and say,

"Well done, my child. Come and take a seat on my <u>left</u> side."

With love, honor, and praise,
Your humble servant

God Has Done Great Things...
Thus, He Has Done
Great Things for Me

If you would take a stroll back in time
Through earlier generations, you will find,
The Lord doing "Great, Miraculous Things,"
From "creation" to this present day and time.

With countless, undeniable testimonies,
Many can solemnly declare "doubt-free."
Stating, if you want to see a miracle,
Take a look at me!

The earth was destroyed by a flood
Thousands of decades ago,
But God gave His word to Noah,
He would not use this action for evermore.

As evidence and proof today
That God doesn't lie,
He made his "promise" through a rainbow
And permanently hung it in the sky.

Because of man's evil and hatred ways
The whole world is under siege.
Everybody, everywhere: rich, poor, colored, or creed,
No one can escape this fatal disease.

Just as God made a commitment to *man*,
Once more, mercy impels Him to make a second amend.
But this time, the role should be reversed by far,
And humanity should make a promise to God.

A commitment to God that establishes enforceable
Laws of equality, freedom, respect, and peace.
To live in harmony with brotherly love,
To reflect "the goodness of what we were created to be."

Then, when we see a rainbow in the sky,
It should also imply:
Thanks for second chances, Lord,
We apologize.

God is the pilot of the super "spreader,"
Spreading healing in all the earth.
He's preparing to do surprisingly "great things"
To restore all nations with a new birth.

If Satan could have his say, he would merely put it this way:

Although I'm the opponent,
I will have to agree,
That "your" Almighty God has also
Done "great things" for me.

He cast me out of heaven but he didn't
Take my roaring power.
Now I can still roam the earth,
Seeking whom I can devour.

He put me in this burning inferno,
But I've managed to stand the heat,
He left me with my screening power,
And I plan to sift you all like wheat.

I can be whatever your weaknesses are,
You see, I have many faces.
Now I'm the ruler of darkness and principalities
My abode is in high places.

Even though I have all these powers,
With "your" God, I just can't defeat,
But until the end, I plan to enjoy
The great things He's done for me!

Thanks for Your Word

Heaven and Earth shall pass away; but my "Word" shall stand.
—Luke 21:33 (KJV)

Thanks for your Holy Spirit, Dear God
    To keep us from going astray.
It has planted a message in our hearts,
    Thy "Word" will guide the way.

With Thy "Word," life was born
    The foundation was laid.
    Man was transformed.

By Thy "Word," the bold became meek
    The lame began to walk.
    The blind began to see.

By Thy "Word," the sunset was delayed.
    The winds stood still.
    Even the seas obeyed.

By Thy "Word," *old man Death* was defeated.
    Your son paid the cost,
    When His mission on earth was completed.

Have Thine own way, Lord, direct us through your "Word"
    Teach the Christians who have found you,
    To save sinners who have not yet heard.

All of our sins can be washed away
>If we would only study the "Word" and believe.
"Thanks" to you for making it simple, Dear God
>For all we need to do is...*r-e-a-d!*

"Study" to show thyself approved unto God...
2 Timothy 2:15 (KJV)

The Writing on the Wall

You better read…

The writing on the wall
You're headed for a fall
You better listen to these facts
It ain't just chicken scratch!

"Writings" are Warnings,
Signs, and Clues,
To lead you, and guide you,
And tell you just what to do.

If you ignore the signs
And fail to take heed,
Your eyes will become so cloudy,
You won't be able to read.

King Belshazzar and his women
Were drinking and having a ball
When *"out"* popped a hand
And wrote some writings on the wall.

The king was so frightened.
He was shaking in his knees.
With all the power he possessed
"This," he could not read!

So he called up Daniel
The wisest of them all.
God would reveal to him
The writings on the wall.

Daniel rushed right over.
He did not hesitate.
He looked at the wall and shook his head.
And this is what he had to say:

Now, King, I know you're anxious
To get this matter cleared,
From what I can see so far,
I don't think you want to hear.

King Nebuchadnezzar, before you,
Brazenly, flaunted and disobeyed
Despite of all the warnings,
He continued his sinful ways.

But just as he was boasting
About his "kingdom divine"
God turned him over
To a "reprobate mind."

He went from "king" to "pauper"
In just one measly hour.
In place of *dining* in the palace
He was *grazing* with the cows.

All of *his misfortunes*
Should have been your "clue" to change.
Instead of straightening up,
You did the same old thing.

Since you made the choice
To follow in his shoes,
This is what the writings
Are saying to you:

- Your days are numbered.
  Right now, there are no more.

- Your works have been weighed.
  And you didn't make the score.

- Your kingdom shall be divided.
  In two different ways.

- Soon and very soon,
  Someone else will take your place!

You better read…

The writing on the wall
You're headed for a fall
You better listen to these facts
It ain't just chicken scratch!

It ain't just chicken scratch!
You better read!

Order My Steps in Your Word

To "Follow the Yellow Brick Road"

When you ask the Lord to "order" your steps, you're asking:
When and where do I begin?
Who do I see?
What course should I take?
What moves should I make?

Sometimes the Lord orders your steps without your asking, because he *detects* and *protects* us through *seen* and *unseen* danger. For instance:

- Have you ever made the wrong turn but ended up in the right place?
- Have you ever been late for an important appointment or a "last chance" situation, but upon arrival, it was detained, postponed, or cancelled in your favor?
- Have you opened a letter that you thought was "junk mail" and found a refund check?
- Have you ever gone on a blind date and met your soul mate?

These are *arrangements* that occur when the *Lord orders your steps*. When your steps are ordered in the word, the road is rewarding, if you obey; although, there may be trouble along the way. Like with Dorothy, in the Wizard of Oz, her instructions were: "Follow the yellow brick road." Simply because Dorothy knew her colors very well, she thought she had it made, but lo and behold, "Danger" became her companion. Nevertheless, she refused to let anything stop her from getting to the Wizard's house because that was her ticket back home.

Life's journey is much the same as Dorothy's. A path of challenging *uncertainties* is destined to come. Therefore, if we want to prevail, we should adhere to similar instructions in the analogy of...

"Follow the Yellow Brick Road"

Numerous times we're tossed *to and fro* by the storms of life. When the dust settles, we often find ourselves alone and/or estranged from friends and family. Moreover, we may be *lost, confused,* and *out of fellowship with God.* We need to find our way back home.

As always in our Christian walk, there will be many obstacles to come our way. In order to claim victory, you need something to win with. For that reason, as you prepare for the journey back home, stop by the Potter's House. He will give you everything you need, and *more*!

Step one: In your present state, you're broken *down*, cracked *up*, stressed *out,* and your whole world is nothing but "pain."
In order to begin this trip back home, you'll need a new way of thinking—a *rejuvenation* of the *brain.*

The Potter will give you a brain with a mind that is well defined.
A mind that will keep you in perfect peace.
A mind that is stayed on Jesus.
Whatsoever is true, whatsoever is pure, whatsoever is honest, whatsoever is lovely, whatsoever is of a good report... a mind that will "think" on these things. Furthermore, when you're down in the dumps, this mind will enable you to *"think yourself happy."*

Step two: On this journey, there's no room for malice, hatred, vengeance, and behaviors of this kind. Surely, a *heart transplant* is definitely in line.

The Potter will take that old "stony" heart, and give you a "clean" heart; one filled with love and compassion.
A heart that will make you love your neighbor as yourself.
A heart that will make you pray for those who despitefully misuse you. A heart that is filled with *unspeakable joy!*
Yes, the Potter will take that "broken" heart and put it back together again.

Step three: Also, on this Christian journey, "*trouble*" is certain and inevitable. To complete this "make-ready" package, you will definitely need great "*courage*."
Courage to *fight the one you cannot see*! (You wrestle not against flesh and blood, but against *principalities, powers, rulers of the darkness,* and *spiritual wickedness* in high places.)
Courage "to fight the giants in your life" *when you only have a pocket full of rocks!*
Courage "to march straight ahead" *when your "river of trouble" is overflowing its banks!*
Courage "to take a stand" when those around you are "staying silent" or turning a death ear!

When at last, the Wizard's house is finally in sight,
There awaits the surprise of your life!
You'll realize this venture was more astounding than one could proclaim, because the *Wizard* and the *Potter* are the same.

He's Alpha and Omega,
The Beginning and the *End*.
He was *there to wave you off* when you started.
When it's over, He's *there to greet you like a Friend*.

Instead of clicking your heels together three times, just give "*three Hallelujah shout-outs*" and you're home!
One for the Father
One for the Son
One for the Holy Ghost

To sum it up and paint the picture clearer, from *a different perspective,* this is how you'll get home:

- That new "rejuvenated" *brain* (with a mind stayed on Jesus) Will get you to *first base.*

- That "pure" *heart* (a sure way to see God) Will take you to *second base.*

- That "double dose" of *courage* (to stand up to the wickedness of this world) Will carry you to *third base.*

- And the Trinity (Father, Son, and the Holy Ghost) Will bring you on home!

"Home plate" is *covered by the Blood.*

Sometimes in life, we barely make it through... we might have to s-l-i-d-e in. But whether you "*slide*" in or have an "easy walk," if you make it safely to the plate...you're home!

You might have to *crawl* in, or *wobble* in, but if you make it safely to the plate...you're home!

Each time you weather a disastrous situation...you're home!

When the doctors scratch their heads in amazement when a fatal disease has disappeared...you're home!

When your children *escape the pressures of gangs, drugs, and teen pregnancy*...you're home!

Each time you *cross* another bridge, *climb* another mountain, or *jump* over another hurdle...you're home!

My advice is to all who have a listening ear:

Let Jesus be your Wizard
No need for *physic friends.*
His Comforter will never leave you.
He'll wash away all of your sins.

When your "steps" are "ordered by the Lord,"
Get ready, the half has never been told.
Trust in His word, obey His commands,
And follow the yellow brick road!

Daniel in the Lion's Den

Listen, people, and listen well!
Here is a hair-raising story to tell!

King Darius favored Daniel
To become head ruler over all
Other governors were jealous
And conspired to plot his downfall.

An "unchangeable" law
Was hurriedly sworn in place
Stating "to kill anyone
Who bowed down to pray."

Now Daniel, a downhearted
Praying man
Said, "Oh, no!"
"I can't follow this plan."

They might be able
To trick the king,
But I'll never go along
With such a crooked scheme.

Not only did Daniel
Refuse to obey
But he kneeled in his window
Praying three times a day.

The officials who colluded
Knew that Daniel wouldn't bend,
They waited anxiously to throw him
Into the *lion's den.*

Daniel's only *defense*
Was a "gentle pat,"
Because God turned that lion
Into a "kitty cat."
Yes! God turned the lion into a kitty cat!

The king was ecstatically happy
To see Daniel still alive.
He fed the governors to the lions
Including their family and wives!

Listen, people, and listen right!
The moral of this story is to stand for Christ!

Don't worry! Don't faint!
Don't even sweat!
Just do your part,
And God will do the rest!

The Mighty Fire

Fire is very hot
As we've been taught.
But I know a *Fire*
That can "cool" you off!

It teaches you a lesson
If you want to learn.
When the flames are real hot,
You won't get burned.

It changes every theory,
Scientist may have thought.
This *Fire's* education
Just can't be bought.

It may be "hot"
Or "not"
When God is calling the shots!

Moses met the *Fire*
In a burning bush.
Something strange was going on,
So he took a closer look.

The fire was blazing,
But the bush was still intact.
Only God above,
Can "glow" a bush like that.

There were three who met the *Fire*
Through a furnace door.
They were Shad-rach, Me-shach,
And A-bed-ne-go.

It was undeniable proof
That the furnace was hot,
Because the guards who threw them in
Burned up on the spot.

The king was astonished
To see the boys so cool.
He saw *Jesus* by their side,
Turning "coals" to "ice cubes."

It may be "hot"
Or "not"
When God is calling the shots!

Women's Liberation

One may ask these questions:

What is this confusion?
Where did it begin?
Who is responsible?
When will it all end?

Only the Lord above can give us the answer,
For now, we cannot see.
We are caught up in this equal rights battle,
And we need Him to be the referee.

Who is responsible?
Could it be the man?
Is he so determined to stay in control
Because he "thinks" this was God's plan?

Or is it because he's afraid,
That if women help share the lead,
They will eventually try to run the whole show,
And maybe they will succeed!

Life's struggles and changing times have forced its way,
Thus making women independently strong.
Could this have created rejection in man's heart
For fear he will no longer be depended upon?

Who is responsible?
Should the woman hold the blame
For wanting to make her own choices,
For having to "share" and "bear" the pain?

For wanting to exercise the right
To do her own decision-making,
As now, in many instances, she has
To help bring home the bacon.

She's spent all these years
Proving that she can.
Just give her a scalpel, hammer, or a gavel,
She can do the job just as well or better than a man.

Maybe the women want to retaliate,
Because they've always kept a mental note
How men have tried to dominate
By preventing them from casting a vote.

The Women's Suffrage Movement in the 1920s
Changed history and paved the way.
Nevertheless, it's over ten decades later.
Women are still fighting for *equal* pay!

What is this evil
That won't bring the two together?
It's making men think they are the best
And having women believe they are better.

Where did it originate?
It maliciously crept into our lives.
It's taken away the identity
Of whom should be the one to provide.

Why did this have to happen?
It has only created a lot of nonsense.

Women still want to be treated like ladies,
But too often, men are reluctant to be gents.

When will all of this end?
Can anyone come up with a date?
Will love survive through this?
Or will it create more hate?

Since no one seems to have the answer,
We will consult our expert referee.
He definitely has the solution to end this mess,
To set our hearts and minds free.

If we turn to God in our most humble way,
These are the words we'll hear him say:

Verily, verily,
I say unto you,
I've designated certain roles
For "man" and "woman" to do.

If everyone would simply manage their own,
My plans won't fail because I'm *never* wrong.
You're both equipped *to balance each other's scale,*
So there's no need for fighting among yourselves.

"Man," keep in mind, I put you in charge of everything that breathes.
Submit yourself to the ways of righteousness,
And you won't become a failure
Like Adam did with Eve.

Love, cherish, and enjoy the *woman,*
She's the "*gift for you,*" I strategically designed.
You're automatically connected to her for life.
She came from the rib in your side.

Virtuous "Woman," you precious stone,
You are an "original" and "one of a kind."
There's no need for you to prove your strengths.
Your purity will let them shine.

Be humble, supportive, and encouraging to "Man."
In you, he will trust and confide.
Don't worry about him putting you behind or under his feet,
Like Adam, he needs you "by his side."

Now, all of this fuss about "Women's Lib"
Has just got to cease!
I intended for you to *complete* each other,
Not *compete!*

It's got you throwing stone for stone,
Saying to each his own,
When you should be trying to seek and find
Ways to liberate your minds.

Respect each other's "worth," I say…
As you *coexist*, find ways to *cooperate*.
Embrace one another's *special* traits.
It'll make this whole world a better place.

Physically, I wanted "woman" to be more delicate,
Wherefore, in skin texture, I made a change.
But your senses and your brains
Are all equally made the same.

With such knowledge, merely put your heads together
And resolve this problem that's causing division and separation.
It's not women's lib you should be worried about.
It's your *eternal salvation!*

I Don't Want Rocks Crying Out for Me

I don't want rocks crying out for me.
I'm going to serve the Lord
And be the "best" that I can be.

He will use something else
To do "whatever" He chooses.
Adhere to wisdom's rules
From the "heavenly host" school.

Learn how God *moves*
Without making a move.
And you will never be *confused*
About *Him* needing *you.*

―――――

He used a *rooster* as a *clock*
To mark the hour.
He used *dry bones* in the valley
Just to show His power.

He used a *whale* as a *ship*
To give Jonah a ride.
He used a *ram* in the *bush*
Just to save a boy's "hide."

He used a *rod* as a *snake*
To offer a plea.
He used *locust* and *frogs*
To bring a king to his knees.

He used a *dove* as a *scout*
To find dry land.
He used *manna* from *heaven*
Just to feed a hungry man.

Let everything that has breath, praise the Lord.
If not…the rocks will take the place of your voice!

The Master Has Done Great Things

One of the *greatest* things
God has "ever" done
Is when He sent us a Savior,
His only Son.

In everyone's heart,
There should be a special song,
To reflect, honor, and give praises
For such a valuable charm.

If you're ever in trouble
And can't seem to make it through,
Just strike up a hymn of that old song,
And it'll tell you what to do.

When you're down and out and filled with despair
Take your burdens to the Lord in prayer
No need to worry or have any doubt,
Just turn it over to the Lord, and *He'll work it out!*

Even the bad things work for good
For those who trust and believe.
He'll pour you out a blessing,
That you won't have room to receive.

Don't let the perils of life

Make you question God with "Why?"
Just keep the faith, *you'll understand it better*
By and by.

There's no need to run,
Just stay in the race,
One day, *"God is going to wipe*
All of your tears away."

Although you might not have riches
And your road is poverty bound,
Be thankful for your health and strength
Because *"the Lord is blessing you right now."*

When everything seems to be failing
And you're defeated on every hand,
Like Gideon, just ask for reassurance.
He'll be your "wet cloth" on "dry land."

He calmed the sea just by waiving His hand
And parked the sun in the sky.
By His command, *dry bones* came alive,
And stood as an army to testify.

Then all men marveled with such remarkable bliss…saying
What manner of man is this?

Just so we'll know
What's yet to come,
God sent a revelation
Through His servant John.

It came as a warning,
Guideline, and mere fact
To show the churches what will happen
If they neglect to stay on track.

There is no reason for anyone
To fail nor be uncertain on what's assigned
Because the Lord has given the test
And revealed the answers at the same time.

He's no crook, but He's coming back
Like a thief in the night.
Take this as an advanced warning.
Get ready for an impromptu sight.

He can't be copied, duplicated,
Nor matched, tit for tat
He is the Almighty, I Am, God
Hallelujah, that settles it!

Keep your eyes toward the hills from whence cometh thy help
And hold fast to God's unchanging hands.
Then surely you will know that He's carrying you
When there're only two footprints in the sand.

Politicians, educators, kings, and queens,
Dance and shout, if you don't have a song to sing.
But in your own special way
Give praises to His name.

For the Master of heaven and earth has done great things!

The Magical Three (3)

Three (3) is a magic charm.
Like the Father, Son, and Holy Ghost
Wrapped up in one.

There were
    Three (3) wise men who went and found my Lord.
    Three (3) temptations that tried to steal his heart.
    Three (3) nights were Jonah in the belly of a whale.

Thirty-three (33) years, Jesus lived!

———

    Three (3) of Jobs friends came to visit him.
    Three (3) Hebrew boys refused to bow before the king.
    Three (3) times denied before the rooster crowed.
    Three (3) days later, Jesus rose!

Three (3)
Is a magic charm.

As

The Father
The Son
The Holy Ghost
Is
The Magical One (1)!

Clichés That Lead Us Astray

A cliché (or quote) is a phrase or thought that may or may not be true. However, we all use them occasionally in general conversation without realizing it; to make a specific point, crack jokes, or for whatever reason. Don't allow yourself to be controlled by "sayings" that usually have a different meaning or effect when it's applied to individual situations. For instance:

(a) *You can't teach an old dog new tricks.* Technology has helped to prove this one wrong.

At the tap of the finger and voice command, the "old dog" *(older folks)* can Skype, Tweet, Text, Snap, take self-ies…you name it!

(b) *Better late than never.* Try using this one on a job interview and your résumé is going straight to "file 13," the trash!

Clichés are overused sometimes, mainly to justify the actions of the "user" as viewed in the following cases.

A Bird in the Hand Is Better Than Two in the Bush

We like to use this cliché because it can be twisted to make us believe that it is better to sit and do nothing, or hold on to what we've got, than to risk losing it all trying to prosper.

In Matthew 25:14–30, the parable of the Talents teaches us that if you don't use it, you will lose it. Jesus gave talents to three men:

One, he gave five talents, another three talents, and the other one talent. The ones with five and three talents displayed gratitude and faith in the Lord; therefore, over a period of several years, they worked hard to utilize and double theirs, so the Lord gave them even more. The one who had only one talent just held on to it and did nothing to better himself; as a result, Jesus decided to take it back.

Don't be afraid to step out on faith, loosen that safety net, or step outside of the box. You should trust God and let go of that *bird* in the hand, because in the end, you will have a whole nest full in the *bush*!

Self-Preservation Is the Law of Nature

This one encourages you to look out for yourself and not be concerned about the cares of others. How can you, as a Christian, not share with your brother who is in a worse situation than you? If you have already acquired financial success, how can you neglect to reach back and give your brother a hand who's trying to climb to the top as well?

In John 13:34, Jesus said, "Love ye one another as I have loved you."

If Jesus had thought only about Himself, He would have come down from the cross, and all souls would be lost. He would not have sent the Holy Spirit to guide, comfort, and keep us.

Furthermore, He pleads our case for forgiveness, continuously, as we sin over and over again. It is a blessing to put others first sometimes, for when you do, God will surely take care of you. He will pour you out a blessing that you won't have room to receive!

The Love of Money Is the Root of All Evil… Money Will Change You

Money can be the start of a new life. Money will change you… as it should. Many times when someone becomes wealthy or successful, out of the ordinary, we have a tendency to believe that he's probably doing something illegal or something has to be "*wrong*." However, this is not necessarily so; it could mean that something is finally "right!" Maybe, "their ship of blessings came in."

Jesus said, "Seek ye first the kingdom of heaven and all things will be added unto you." *Money* and *wealth* are also included. Job was one of the richest men of his time, but he was also a righteous man. During the course of time, he lost his health and all his earthly possessions, absolutely "everything." However, Job proved that the *love of money* didn't change his love for God, and in return for his trustworthiness, he was given everything back threefold. So bear this in mind, money "can" change you; just don't let it "shortchange" you.

All Work and No Play Makes Jack a Dull Boy

We like to use this cliché because it gives a *justifiable* pass to slack off as needed! It allows us to believe that unless we mix a little "fun" in our routine of going to work and church, we will be unhappy or out of touch with society. In spite of that, when you're *working* for Jesus, it's an ongoing process, but you can balance the two with ease. You'll be able to manage social life, family time, and a job without feeling depressed or bored. There's never a "dull" moment as follows:

- Every time you encourage a backslider to return to church, you're *working* for Jesus.
- Anytime you give a testimony to encourage some lost soul to have faith and trust in the Lord, that's *working* for Jesus.
- When you perform random acts of kindness or good deeds in any fashion, that's *working* for Jesus.

This type of work is effortless yet rewarding? What's *dull* about putting a little sunshine in someone's life?

Again, you can see that when *working* for the Lord, "play" is already incorporated in the "work" because it's *fun* being a blessing to someone. What's implied to be *dull* is pure *joy*. It is a joy to know that each time when *one* soul is saved, all of heaven shouts with joy!

Innocent until Proven Guilty

We all are guilty of wrongdoings…lying, cheating, stealing, among others; however, unless you're exposed, you hide behind the cliché: "innocent until proven guilty." While you are comfortable in your "sin skin," be reminded that Romans 3:23 (NIV; emphasis added) says, "We're *all guilty of sin*, and have fallen short of the glory of God." This scripture declares that because of sin, we are automatically in the "guilty" category and *cannot be proven innocent.*

Knowing that we are already cursed by sin, God has given us another way out through *grace* and *mercy.* This avenue alone should urge you to do away with the cliché and strive for the "mercy seat." There is nothing that describes *deliverance* better than the grace of God. You *can't buy it;* you *can't win it;* you *can't even earn it*! It's a priceless *present* from *The Great I Am.* Above any and every thing you might "think" you need, God has profoundly stated, "My grace is sufficient!

The DeGreprobate State(s)

Definitions

A reprobate mind—to condemn strongly as unworthy, unacceptable; a depraved, unprincipled or wicked person. A person rejected by God.

Grace—unmerited favor; the *undeserved fovor of God* toward human-kind; a *supernatural advantage* for a successful life; *a gift from God.* (Sin has condemned us to death, but by "grace," we shall live.)

*Gre-pro-bate—A "reprobate" *saved by* "grace."
(Example: King Nebuchadnezzar—Daniel 4:28–36)

*De-Gre-pro-bate—A "reprobate" *who has run out of "grace"!* No more favors! Doomed to die! Done!
(Example: Saul— (1 Samuel 16:13–14), (1 Samuel 18:12), (1 Samuel 28:6), (1 Samuel 28:15–20)

The DeGreprobate State(s)

*DeGreprobate "state of mind"—The condition or character of a DeGreprobate's thoughts or feelings.

*DeGreprobate "state of residence"—The "state" where a DeGreprobate resides.

   *Note: The terms and definitions were created by the writer.

The "Fate Timeline" of a DeGreprobate

One Who Runs Out of Grace

I. God gets fed up!

- Turns His back
- Washes His hand
- Shuts His eyes and ears
- Allows Satan to have his way

II. Grace is used up!

- Third strike—game over
- No more time on the clock
- All she wrote!

III. Skid row is destined.

- Down-bounded
- Gloom-doomed
- Destruction under construction

IV. A "miserable" journey

- The journey is like traveling on a rugged road in an uncovered wagon, in the desert, in the heart of the heat months, with no water… If the *noise* and *bumps* won't get you, the *dust, heat,* and *a dry mouth of thirst* most definitely will.

- Imagine being stranded in deep waters during stormy weather, in a *canoe with no oars*…you are literally "up the creek without a paddle"; it *keeps downpouring, non-stop*, all the time.

State of Residence

At the state line entrance, the danger signs
Are flashing and posted all about.
Carelessly, no one heeds the warning:
Only "one way in" and "no way out!"

In this state, "dog eat dog"
Is a natural way of living.
Everybody is taking,
And *no one* is giving!

Get ready to wander in confusion
As your road gets dimmer day by day.
The Lord has taken His lamp from your feet,
Which turned off the light in your pathway.

Those days of "*call Him up* and *tell Him what you want*"
Will soon become faded memories in time.
You won't be able to get in touch with God anymore.
He's disconnected your communication lines.

All appeals and petitions are nonnegotiable.
There's no need to cry, plead, or beg.
Right before God turned his back on you,
He removed your protective hedge.

Every person you meet is a liar and deceiver.
They don't know the meaning of *the truth*.
You can't trust not one of them.
All the same, no one can trust *you*.

The only laws are the "outlaws!"
There are no rules or regulations.
The "verdict" is always "guilty,"
With a "death" sentence or incarceration.

They routinely practice
Their *Golden Rule:*
"Do unto others
Before they do unto you."

It's understandable that the houses
Are built on shaky, unstable land,
Because, without God's foundation,
All grounds are sinking sand.

No one feels free to drive their cars.
In fact, it's much safer to crawl,
In hope to escape those pot holes
That corroded into endless "pitfalls."

Those high-minded expensive car owners
Have never been seen again.
The streets near their homes are all *one way,*
And they all have "*dead*" ends.

State of Mind

In this state,

There are no morals,
And no shame.
Everybody is turned loose
To do their own thing.

They call themselves the "New World,"
Disregarding the *Bible* and *God's man/woman creation.*
Any scripture that is unacceptable for them
Is rewritten to fit their own interpretation.

Child pornography and pleasures of the flesh
Are the norm for having fun.

Fathers are sleeping with daughters,
And mothers are going with their sons.

"Meth" and "crack" are the choices for dope,
But *any* drug available is a good pick.
Addicts sit on the corner like scum of the earth,
Waiting for the next "fix" or "trick."

When you're all alone in trouble, save your voice.
Despite an intensive cry, nobody will *come* to help.
Unlike The Prodigal Son, who slept with hogs,
You won't have sense enough to *come* to yourself.

Conclusion

The other side of the fence may look greener,
But it's nothing but "Bermuda grass."
As soon as you cut down one problem,
Another pops up, only twice as bad.

If financial loss, a broken heart, or such problems arise,
Don't turn to drugs or witchcraft, just to name some.
Be still, be patient, and always trust in God.
Like Job, your *change* will surely come.

You might have to suffer many times,
But there's a rewarding relief for strife.
Jesus is the perfect example
That suffering is eternal life.

Stay in the race, hold on to the end,
Especially when all hope is gone.
It might be slow going, but don't give up,
Unfaltering *endurance* is how the race is won.

Wait for answers; wait for renewed strength
When burdens get heavy and times are hard.
You will walk and not faint, nor get weary,
If you just "wait!" Wait on the Lord.

The angels are pleading "for heaven's sake,"
Stay in fellowship with *mercy* and *grace*.
Don't let "death," *the ultimate fate,*
Greet you…in a DeGreprobate "state"!

Sleep Tight

Between the "tick" and the "tock,"
God is always "in" time and on the "dot."
He sees your pain.
He's aware that you're mentally drained.

He alone knows "exactly"
What you're going through,
And He can "instantly"
Turn your grayest sky, blue!

As a consoling reminder
In your moment of despair,
Cast your burdens on the Lord
And leave them there!

While you're juggling, multitasking,
And overcome by the problems of others,
God, who specializes in "everything,"
Is exclusively tending to *your* troubles.

Go to sleep
Have a restful nap
Wake up refreshed
God's got your back!

It'll be all over by the morning light.

Sleep Tight!

Holidays
and Special
Occasions

'Twas the Day before Christmas

'Twas the day before Christmas,
And all through the church
Everyone was scrambling
To get there first.

They were excited and anxious
For what was about to take place.
A variety of "surprises,"
Leading up to the *big day*.

The children were dressed in costumes
And the grownups were too.
Setting the stage for the miracle
That became the Living Truth.

Now Dancers! And Prancers!
Swirled gracefully in form
As the holy choir stood unified
To deliver a host of songs.

Rejoice! The choir director proclaimed!
Stand on your feet and praise His name.
Give ye heed to what I say
Christ is born this Christmas Day.

Everyone was attentive
To see the celebration flow.

The song "Infant Holy"
Really "stole the show."

The leaders sang powerfully, a vivid call,
"For His bed a cattle stall."
The congregation was clapping and having a ball
Praising, *Christ the Babe is Lord of all.*

The choir sang backup
With a smooth Gospel groove,
Adding a special touch
With doo, doo, doo, doo, doop!

And to the crowd's most joyous delight,
A special tribute to the birth of Christ,
"Hark! The herald angels sing."
"Christ is born in Bethlehem."

Then in a twinkle, praise dancers entered
With movements that touched them all,
Trying to express with explicit emotions
What Jesus Christ shall be called.

He's Alpha and Omega, the Beginning and the End.
He's the immaculate "everything" in between.
Wonderful, Counselor, Mighty God, Prince of Peace,
He's the Everlasting Father and *King of Kings.*

By this time, the pastor
Just couldn't hold his seat.
If only for a few moments,
He just had to preach!

He started with the truth that's in his heart.
"I worship the One who is born the Son of God."

He has come to bring us joy, power and peace.
He did all of this for little ole me.

He reminded us to "stick to the script"
And be careful not to lose sight.
That the *real* reason we celebrate
Is to honor *the Bread of Life.*

The *main* character
Sent down from Glory.
Nothing else is needed.
Jesus is *the whole story.*

As the curtains closed on the occasion, like times before,
The Angelic choir sang just once more.
Then, I heard the pastor exclaim with pure dynamic cheer!
Merry Christmas to all, and to all a Happy New Year!

Dad
A Father's Day Salute

When you are a young child,
Your dad is the strongest of them all,
So big, so mighty,
So tall.

If there is a problem,
He can quickly lick it.
If a toy is broken,
He can easily fix it.

You can crawl all over him,
And he won't complain.
You can run through his pockets
And take all the loose change.

Without a doubt,
"Your" dad outshines the most!
Watching his actions unfold,
He's your superhero!

But somewhere through the middle school years,
Things begin to change.
All fathers start to "look"
And "sound" the same.

They all play the same "broken record"
And snap to the same old beat.

Just check out this list of tunes,
And you'll see what I mean.

Tune 1: When I was your age...
Tune 2: Don't let me have to come in there...
Tune 3: Money don't grow on trees...
Tune 4: If you want rights, get a job and pay some bills...
Tune 5: As long as you live in *this* house...
Tune 6: Eleven o'clock doesn't mean 11:05!

After hearing these tunes
Over and over again,
You wonder if you can make it
Without going insane!

But when you're older
And really understand,
You look back and say
My daddy was "the man."

Sometimes he preached,
And sometimes he fussed,
But "all the times" he wanted
What was best for us.

So, to all the fathers
On your special day,
Thanks for your guidance
And for showing us the way.

I'm sure when we're grown up
And have children of our own,
We'll use the same lyrics
Of your same old songs.

Happy Fathers' Day!

Mother, You're Every Woman
A Mothers' Day Salute

You're the last one to eat.
You get the least amount of sleep.
You're up by the crack of dawn.
You've laid out a meal
And washed the clothes.
All, before the rising of the sun.

"Bionic Woman" is just the title
That you can easily claim.
You spread yourself incredibly thin,
Without showing any pain.

"Remember to do this."
And "don't forget that."
Make sure to "write it down."
And "remember where it's at."

Your mind is often in "overdrive,"
Planning the day like a map.
With all this mental strain,
You've earned your own "thinking cap."

As much as you run,
You are the greatest "track star."
Soccer games, band practice,
You make a taxi out of the car.

Like "Superman," you're always,
"Johnnie on the spot,"
Transforming to fix the problem
Whether it's serious or not.

From scraped knees to nose bleeds,
High fever, or the flu,
"Dr. Mom," you deserve your license
Because you always know what to do.

So, on this special occasion,
We salute your many hats.
Today, you deserve a "halo,"
Because an "angel," you're truly that!

Happy Mother's Day!

A Prayer of Blessings on "Fathers' Day"

Our Heavenly Father,

In Your Son Jesus's name, we're sending an emergency call to heaven for a "special blessing request." Father, this request is extremely urgent. We're asking you to put your present calls on hold and stop all incoming calls. This exceptional day has been set aside specially to honor fathers. They all would like to be recognized and have a joyous time on "their" day. Many of them will be disappointed and miss their blessing without realizing the reason why for the mere fact that they do not acknowledge you nor do they understand the qualities of a real father. Therefore, the Women's Ministry has taken it upon ourselves to send a plea on their behalf. We're asking for "special blessings," Lord—not just for "special fathers" in particular but for all fathers: the Good, the Bad, and the Ugly.

There are the "good" fathers who are the sole providers for their families. The ones who teaches their children right from wrong; how to love, share, and respect one another; even to love you, dear Lord, whom they have never seen; the ones that set a good Christian example for his children to follow. The ones who spend individual time with each child, taking in account their unique personalities.

Lord, grant these fathers your "supreme" blessing. Please honor them with an extraordinary measure of your "automatic reward" for their good deeds that were done in secret. Please increase their faith with multiple blessings of encouragement, inspiring them to trust in your word and "stay the course" even when difficulties or obstacles may prevent things from going as planned. Lastly, as an added bonus, please make this Fathers' Day unforgettable! Give them an experience of "unspeakable joy" with all of their favorite things!

Then, there are the "bad" fathers who put all the responsibilities on the mothers. They won't keep a steady job. They have poor work habits, hostile attitudes, take excessive days off from work, anger management problems, and the list goes on. They have "built-in," "cop-out" excuses to avoid having to man up and do what's necessary to take care of their families. They are the ones who make a paycheck every week but will gamble it off or drink it up and come short of their duties and responsibilities. The ones who disrespects his wife and children with foul and abusive language; the ones who just walk off from their children and never look back.

Lord, for these deadbeat fathers, we're asking for a "triple dose" blessing. Please, give them an "extra-strength, fast-acting, time-released" portion of your blessings. Please, inspire their hearts and minds to seek your face. Prove to them with overwhelming blessings and life-changing experiences that they can always lean and depend on you. Shower them with your loving kindness despite their irresponsible ways. Please lead and guide them with knowledge and understanding to see that "any day" can be a "new day" for them to live up to the title "head of household." Give them a "wow" factor moment to show that good things "can" happen to those who make bad choices.

Then Lord, there are the "ugly" fathers. They are the kind that will do well but just won't do right. They are good providers and hard workers, but it stops right there. They won't get involved in their children's school activities nor seize the opportunity to spend quality time with other family endeavors. They'd rather spend their leisure time on the golf course, at the sports arena, or working out at the gym as such. Minor repairs, such as leaky faucets, a broken toilet seat, or a clogged garbage disposal, are left undone for an extreme length of time. They will attend church services occasionally, but only when it's not football season.

Lord, for these "wishy-washy" fathers, we're asking for a stronger blessing than before. They're neither hot nor cold, and we know you'd rather spew them out of your mouth. Even so, on the other hand, with a little spiritual guidance and the studying of your word, they can become good candidates for leadership positions with social events as well as the church. Opportunities are always available for chaperones, volunteer engagements, and many other rewarding involvements.

Bless them, oh Lord, to know that it takes more to being a father than just paying the bills. Please make them aware of the effectiveness of their actions to take a Christian stand to fulfill their moral and legal obligations. Not only will the family benefit but the whole community as well. Please help them to develop the type of character that is encouragement for other fathers as well as good role models for upcoming young men. Besides, what is greater and more gratifying than to earn the respect of your wife, children, and to get a pat on the back from your Heavenly Father.

Lord, we thank you for honoring our high-priority prayer request with your "undivided attention." We know that you are the Almighty God with powers to hear, see, and do "everything" for "everybody" at the same time. Nevertheless, you displayed your warmest devotion and gave a special listening ear to our prayers and concerns for fathers throughout the world. For this, we are most grateful. We're hanging up now, because we know there are other calls waiting to "finally" get through. But just in case we left someone out...for future guidance and fathers-to-be, please implant this thought into every man's heart and soul: You have allowed them to wear Your title, "Father," which is the first of the Trinity, and it should be worn with dignity and respect. Therefore, whatever they undertake, it is a "reflection on Your name."

We ask these blessings in Jesus's name. Amen.

One Little Thing

For your Birthday...

I bought one little thing
You can really use.
No food, no clothes,
No fancy shoes.

Just a little something
You really need
To help you navigate
From Point "A" to "B."

And if you're wondering
"What could this possibly be?"
Look inside
To see if you don't agree.

Happy Birthday!
(Gas gift card)

People, Special Request, and Special Occasions

Rev. Joe Dean Johnson

A Devoted Shepherd of God
Pastor of the Riceville Mount Olive Baptist Church
Houston, Texas
For forty-two years (1967–2009)

One of the most kind, wise, and humble spiritual leaders
Who served in the Kingdom of God.

Retired as Riceville Pastor Emeritus
Called to glory in June 2014

Joe D.

Joe *Dean* Johnson is his birth name.
He's distinguished and unique.
Just for an instant, with honor and respect,
He's kindly referenced as "*Joe D.*"

Some theologians take great pride
In how they are perceived.
Dr. "This" and Father "That,"
And a list of all their degrees.

Some of these titles are honorable,
And honor should be given indeed.
But there are others that are mere flattery,
Which tends to mislead and deceive.

But here is one, whose most concerns
Are saving souls and helping those in need.
He's at his best in his meekest element,
Just being plain old *Joe D.*

If you really want to know
What forms this tree,
Take a quick glimpse
From the head to the feet.

Wisdom, knowledge, and observant
Describe his mind as a start.

Add loyal, compassion, kindness, and love
To show the mechanics of his heart.

Include honesty, fair, and righteousness
To express his natural-born demands.
Mixed well with humble, faithful, and obedience
Yields the product of a God-fearing man.

He walks a little slow and speaks very low,
But don't let the gentle pace confuse you.
During service, when it appears that he's napped too long.
He'll rise and preach a summary of every song.

He doesn't "sugarcoat" or "dress up" the truth
Because the "truth" is what sets you free.
Adultery, shacking up, and same-sex lifestyles
Are just a few of his specialties.

When it comes to settling disputes,
He's careful not to take sides.
His ultimate "answer" is "to do what's right"
And let God be the one to decide.

Some thinks, because he's so humble,
That he's quiet and no fun at all.
But my advice is to have a "one-on-one."
Then afterward, you make the call.

Compared to many other pastors,
His salary is only a small fee.
Nevertheless, if there was no pay at all,
He would preach just as hard for free.

He's a peculiar old fellow, no doubt,
But he's very easy to figure out.

If you know anything about Christ,
This is the one he strives to be like.

While guiding, leading, and
Watching over God's sheep,
He preaches, teaches, and holds steadfast
To the Bible and his Christian beliefs.

His status is a perfect example
For all ministers to take a stand,
To be careful not to lower God's standards
For the benefits and acceptance of man.

If there was such an optical device
As a "divine futurescope,"
One could zoom straight into heaven
To see whose name is on the role.

If all the names were listed by rank,
This is what you would clearly see,
An *empty space* between "Job" and "Daniel"
Marked: <u>Honorably Reserved for *Joe D.*</u>

Excerpts and Words of Wisdom

From the Sermons of Pastor Johnson

(A good old "country" Southern Baptist preacher)

Sermons

1. *It's in There!*

    Whatever you need, it's in the Bible.
    If you want to know how to treat your

    A. Neighbor? It's in there… Love thy neighbor as thyself.
    B. Parents? It's in there… Honor thy father and thy mother.
    C. Children? It's in there… Spare the rod, and spoil a child; do not provoke your children to wrath, but bring them up in the training and admonition of the Lord.
    D. If you still do not understand what to do…*just trust in the Lord with all your heart and lean not to your own understanding; in all your ways, acknowledge Him* and *He will direct your path.*

2. *Something to Win With*

    We are all given a talent.

    A. Some work with their hands, like a mechanic or builder.

B. Some use their knowledge and brains, such as a scientist or lawyer.

C. Others may have a *gift of service* to work with people with special needs, like a caregiver or missionary.

All these talents are "*extra!*" The main thing we all have to "win with" is Jesus Christ. The whole world can be against you, but *when you accept Jesus as your personal Savior, "you" have something to win with!*

Words of Wisdom

1. *Slop talk*—a sample story about taking hogs to the slaughter.

A. Do not feed *slop* to your most prized commodity.

B. There is a benefit to feeding the hog with special corn and grains:

> (1) The quality of the meat is better.
> (2) You get more money for the hog.

C. Main point: Do not let anyone feed you *slop*.
    Such as

- Internet/social media
- Friends
- TV ministry
- Family members
- Church members

D. Follow the Bible and you can't go wrong. The Scriptures states, "Study to show thyself approval."

2. *Milk glass advice*

- Be careful how you preach and teach to others about righteous living when you're guilty of the same or similar things.
- Your message is equivalent to giving water in a milk glass.
- Your image is automatically tarnished.
- Whatever you say will look "cloudy," "shady," and won't mean a hill of beans.

3. *Short cover*

- There is no magic way to cover up sin because the Bible clearly warns, "*Your sins will find you out!*" In other words, *you will be exposed.*
  It's the same as using *short cover.*
- When you pull the cover up to your head…your feet are out.
- When you cover up your feet…the top part of your body is out. You're still uncomfortable!

You can't win—you're *exposed* one way or the other.

4. *Lending money*

- Do not lend money that you will need for your personal well-being. If the money is not paid back, it won't put you in a bind, and you and the person who borrowed the money won't have to "fall out" about it, especially if they are a friend.
- For instance, do not lend money you are going to need for your car payment, rent/ mortgage, utilities, or other important necessities.

5. *Hold up "your" corner*

- Anything can be accomplished if everyone would just hold up their corner.
- In other words, if a group effort is required to perform a task, there is no room for "slacking." If each of you would just do "your" part, it will work just fine.
- Picture four people carrying something heavy on a four-cornered board; *if either one of them let go of their corner,* the object will easily slide off.

6. *Whosoever you help, God or Satan will win*

Whenever crucial decisions arise in your life concerning doing right or wrong (for whatever reason), "you" have the power to predict the outcome by the choice you make: You can "either reap the benefit or suffer the consequence" because "you" are the deciding factor.

Whichever way you choose, it's going to be two against one, and the two are going to win.

- If you choose to do wrong, then evil will win because that's you and Satan against God.

- If you choose to do right, righteous is going to win. That's you and God against Sin.

It boils down to asking yourself, *whose side are you on?*

Pastor Johnson's Sense of Humor

7. *Holding a grudge*

It is better not to hold a grudge against someone because *every time you see that person, you will have to get mad all over again.*

8. *Adultery and fornication*

- Do not take pleasure in wallowing in sin...cheating, slipping, and tipping.

- You should feel so sorrowful, and your conscience should bother you so bad until you would want to hide your face or fall on your knees and beg God's forgiveness.

- But instead of feeling guilty, you walk away whistling, strutting, and "picking your teeth."

9. *A wandering mind during church service*

In order *to get something out of the service*, you have to *bring something to the service.* Often times you cannot stay focused because your mind is everywhere, except church—boredom, distractions, humorous and ugly thoughts, or your interest is just plainly on other things.

If an announcement was made, stating, "Whatever you're thinking will flash up on a screen, and scroll around for everyone to see," the church would be cleared out within seconds!

For example: Just imagine, the thoughts along with the person's name, appearing on the screen as follows:

- "Now look at this young lady, she is revealing too much in church, and that loud red dress is too tight and too short."—Ms. Lucinda

- "Ooh, she is hot in that tight red dress. It makes my temperature rise. Please, please, come to the front row so I can get a better look."—Jacen

- "Yep, I'll just go to the restroom and sneak right on out the back door. I should be able to catch the second half of the football game."—Will

- "Roberta needs to sit her old self down, with that pink hair and those windshield wiper eyelashes. She looks a hot mess trying to act young."—Sister Pauline

- Worst of all, the person sitting next to "you" will know exactly what "you" thought about their foul breath and what it smells like!

We're all guilty of letting our minds drift into daring places "during church service."

The Makings of You: Annotation

This poem is a tribute to the "Call to Ministry."

Reverend Curtis Ray Lucas has now been in the ministry for thirty-eight years, since December 6, 1982, and have pastored for thirty-six years. He's been married for fifty blissful years. To this union are four children, three daughters and one son. He's a doting grandpa of twenty-two grand and great-grand-children combined.

When asked, how he wants to be remembered, four words simply said it all: "I love the Lord!"

A Dedication

To my beloved cousin, with whom I am well pleased… Curtis Lucas.

These are: THE MAKINGS OF YOU

Your father would have been proud in his last days
If he could have seen what was up ahead.
But nevertheless, who's to say
That he's not listening from the dead.

For some strange reason, "Preacher"
Is what his name came to be
Not realizing that he'd be the producer
Of one in reality.

Maybe this was God's special way
Of giving a future clue.
Undoubtedly the seed was spiritually blessed,
To originate *the makings of you*.

From early childhood, you learned to work
On a farm where you mastered many tools.
From planting the grain, to harvesting it again,
You even had to miss days from school.

But there's no need to fret or even regret
Your days of "little boy blue."
Because these times helped to cultivate
The makings of you.

Now you are a man and have been blessed
With a family and a home.
And by each member,
You're highly depended upon.

From the one that's not walking
To the one who does too much talking.
From the one that always seem to trip or fall,
To the one who knows it all!

Who on earth could have put together
A more perfect troop.
So praise God for the offspring from
The makings of you.

Since it was God who gave you life,
You've shown thanks by giving it back in return,
Because you know His reward is greater
Than any earthly honors you could ever earn.

Although you've taken that giant step,
God is still not through.
This is only the beginning of the second half of
The makings of you.

Mr. Short Stuff: Annotation

Mr. C. was overly round in the middle and short in statue, but the love and respect for his jolly personality and pleasant demeanor would override any "shortcomings." He was a workaholic, juggling long hours on another job in his spare time as anyone could expect, by him having *twelve children*. Greater opportunities became available which prompted him to leave the company three months shy of one year of service. He was a devoted husband and loving father, with one little hilarious flaw... He was a "girl watcher" with no apologies. Everyone in the whole company who knew Mr. C. was aware of his subtle mannerism.

It became an "inside joke" until "the reveal" at the roast.

The poem was reviewed by employees of Mr. C.'s immediate unit for approval, and they all unanimously agreed that it was a perfect portrayal of his character. At the farewell luncheon, they waited anxiously to see the reaction from the crowd. The stage was set. All the "big wheels" were there, president, vice president, supervisors, etc. Throughout the whole reading, the room was filled with laughter and high fives. Practically everyone, including Mr. C. was red in the face with tears rolling down their cheeks from laughing so hard! The humor of it all was taken in stride. The poem was on target and became *the highlight of the party!*

Mr. Short Stuff

(A Farewell Roast)

"Short" must be your only style!
Because you were here for just a *short* while.
If your stay with us could have been measured by time,
We would have known back in January, your height would only take
you to nine (months).

Only the "tall"
Could have lasted through twelve.
But with a short fellow like you,
No one would be able to tell.

Of course we know that twelve was "not"
One of your missing "shots,"
Because twelve of "your" times in bed
Created twelve more heads!

We made a few plans for you,
Though now, it doesn't matter.
The guys had decided to all pitch in
And buy you a stepladder.

The ladies in the cubicles were afraid
You might get excited and fall.
So they thought it would be much safer
To have them lower the wall.

We didn't bother to get your approval on this
Because we knew you'd like the idea just fine
In that way, you could fix your coffee
And view the ladies at the same time.

You need not leave a photograph
To remind us in the days to come.
For your "special uniqueness" was noticed
And will be remembered by everyone.

We will remember your silent grin
Every time a sexy woman walks in.
We will remember the twinkle in your eye
If her skirt should happen to fly.

We will remember the quick
And sudden change in your mood
Every time we see a stuffed turkey
Or an abundance of food.

So you see, you'll be remembered
In many different ways.
For your legendary actions
Will linger on for days and days

After all is said and done,
Our experience with you
Was hard work
Wrapped up in fun.

Having you as our leader
Has really been a pleasure.
You've shown us more concernment
Than any scale, meter, or ruler could measure.

Although your appearance is short and small
Your wide-range kindness has touched us all.
At this time, we want to wish you much success
And the best of luck.

Goodbye and may God bless you,
Mr. Short Stuff!

The Big "Five-O": Annotation

Turning fifty is a life-altering change from "young" to "not as young anymore." (The term *old* is unacceptable at this point.)

U pon special request, this poem was exquisitely tailored for Faye Dunwood's Fiftieth Birthday Celebration. This is definitely a commemorative keepsake to reflect on such an *unforgettable milestone* occasion.

The Big "Five-O"

Mother Nature has been kind to me,
From the very first day I was born
Jack Frost laid a blanket in snow white
On a crisp October morn.

The trees dressed up in reddish browns
To carefully paint the scene
As the world received another angel
Ready to spread its wings.

Mother Nature has been kind to me,
As the seasons of life brought change.
She laid the grounds for my family tree
So did the part of my last name.

The sea of love overflowed
And offered its most prime catch
The stars sent sprinkles of moon dust
To ordain my perfect match.

Mother Nature has been kind to me
For how she cultivated my seed
That yielded two beautiful offspring
What a wonderful crop to reap!

I was showered with more happiness
Than I could ever imagine it to be.

Now, twice I've shared my mother's joy
When she first laid eyes on me.

Mother Nature has been kind to me.
I've weathered the storms and fears.
But now it's up to Father Time
To take hold of my "golden years."

Soon the snow will dwell on my roof,
And the twinkle in my eye disappears.
I will graciously accept the change
And look forward to the "silver years."

Now the hour glass is still half full
And my life is rich yet "thrifty."
I'd like to give thanks to Father Time
For the opportunity to celebrate *fifty*!

It's Your Twenty-Fifth Anniversary! (Annotation)

Kevin Green is a loyal husband, dedicated father, family-oriented, and just an amazing all-around guy. His mother, Rayla, wanted to honor her "first born" in a distinctive and notable way. She decided to add a little *spice* to his "twenty-fifth wedding anniversary bash" with a *live presentation* of an original poem to share among family and guests.

Unexpectedly, to Kevin and his wife, Andrea, the "spice" would include a humorous "dash" of *their excessive behaviors*. However, it was a joyous "element of surprise"!

It's Your Twenty-Fifth Anniversary!

After twenty-five years, you still proclaim
To be the perfect soul mates.
Instituted and ordained by God, himself,
You're unmistakably each other's fate.

Only through the will of God could you tolerate,
Compensate, and merely look the other way
To put up with each other's little *pet peeves*
On a year-after-year basis.

He runs the house
Like a military dorm.
The only thing that's missing
Is the proper uniforms.

She has clearly earned the title
Of the "online ordering queen"
With so many weekly packages,
The doorstep looks like a postal scene.

The "power" and "magic" of your love
Was God's gift, as a guide,
To nurture and cultivate *the union*
To keep you by each other's side.

The "power" of love
Makes you anxious to come home.

The "magic" of love
Prevents the thought of wanting to roam.

The "power" of love
Keeps the marriage wheel turning.
The "magic" of love
Keeps the "fireworks" coming!

Twenty-five years and counting,
With each day, a new start,
To fall in love over and over again
Until death do you part.

Happy Anniversary!

More than a Woman to Me (Annotation)

Annie Agusta Kleinpeter

This was a fashionable way to honor "The Poet," with a "poem" from her loving daughter, Anita. Born Annie Agusta Webb, she was the oldest of five children. She graduated from G.W. Griffin High School in Lake Providence, LA. She attended Grambling College (now Grambling State University) and majored in English. An avid reader, she also had a passion for writing and reciting poetry; however, her poems have not been published yet.

She and her husband Curtis Kleinpeter Sr. had twelve children together. They were staunch believers in the Lord, Jesus Christ, and instilled the same spiritual values in their children, thus encouraging them to obtain a higher education beyond high school.

More than a Woman to Me

From the eyes of a child,
Her mom is the best.
She is always that extra-everything
Far more than all the rest.

Despite all of her shortcomings,
She manages to feel your heart with glee.
Here are only a few reasons why my
Mom is more than a woman to me.

Although she holds no PhD
Or any kind of bachelor's degree,
She spreads her knowledge in twelve directions
Through the roots of her family tree.

From scrubbing floors to washing doors,
Her quest was one big expectation
That her children would share from her despair
The benefits of a college education.

Comparing her life to the universe,
She's been that Evening Star,
To guide us and direct us
Which made us who we are.

Though sickness prevailed over her body
She's been the backbone of the clan.

Like a miracle, when her siblings would fall,
She, then, became their right hand.

More precious than any jewel
She's rare and hard to find.
Like an uncut diamond, her expressions lie dormant
In masterpieces of rhythm and rhyme.

How on earth could one person sustain the pain
Of so many, I'll never be able to see.
But one thing for sure, no one can ever be
The woman she is to me.

The Greatest Champ Annotation

Cassius Marcellus Clay Jr. was born in Louisville, Kentucky, on January 14, 1942. The renowned Cassius Clay made his professional boxing debut against Tunney Hunsaker in October 1960, winning the bout in six rounds. He changed his name to Muhammad Ali in 1964 after converting to Islam. On February 25, 1964, *Ali won the heavyweight championship title after defeating the eminently favored Sonny Liston* in six rounds.

I n 1967, Ali refused to be drafted into the Army because of religious and political beliefs. He was stripped of his world heavyweight title and his license to box. Nevertheless, Ali persevered. Three years later in 1970, his boxing license was reinstated. The following year, in 1971, his conviction was also overturned in a unanimous decision.

Meanwhile, Joe Frazier, Ali's most fierce rival, had been crowned heavyweight champion in 1968 while Ali was banned from boxing. In 1971, Ali was on his thirty-second winning streak when he was defeated by his most bitter opponent, Joe Frazier. This bout was called the Fight of the Century, but it also became the *shock of the century*. It was painful for the world to witness a beloved and admired champ lose the battle. But Ali bounced back with a series of awesome wins that demonstrated the *champ* was still on track. In 1973, *Joe Frazier was dethroned by George Foreman.*

In 1974, *Muhammad Ali went on to become heavyweight champion again in a title fight against George Foreman*, known as the *Rumble in the Jungle* (Zaire, Africa). In 1975, still dissatisfied and wanting to prove to the world that he deserved to hold the undisputed heavyweight crown, Joe Frazier challenged Ali to a *third match*, referred to as the *Thrilla in Manila* (Quezon, Philippines). This fight was the final showdown to break the tie! It was a brutal and grueling fourteen rounds of pure resentment in every form. Frazier got the best of Ali in the middle, but Ali got the best of him at the beginning and end, where it counted the most. Frazier's horrifying swollen eyes distinctly impaired his vision to a point where he appeared to be stumbling in the dark. Fearing a devastating outcome, Frazier's chief second, Eddie Futch, asked the referee to stop the fight after the fourteenth round. Ali won by a technical knockout (TKO).

In 1978, Muhammad Ali, age thirty-six, defeated Leon Spinks, age twenty-four, to become the *first fighter to win the world heavyweight championship for the third time in his career.* Ali's boxing record, along with his character, charisma, and the manner in which he dominated the sport, sets him apart from all others of his caliber.

Many boxing commentators and historians give recognition to Muhammad Ali *as the greatest heavyweight boxer of all time.*

The Greatest Champ
Poem Annotation

I've always been a huge fan of Muhammad Ali since junior high. Despite the negative publicity, controversy, and consequences he endured, my love and admiration never wavered. He will always be my hero.

T his poem is very special to me because it was written as a project for an English class in the '70s, when I was a student in college. (Of course I got an "A" and "thumbs up" from the teacher, as she stopped in her tracks to read it silently in front of the class). Throughout the years, I've yearned for the moment of opportunity when Ali would read the contents, feel the genuine love in the lyrics, and see how the *perception of his greatness* remains the same over decades-long. Several attempts were made to reach him, but to no avail. Now he has a world of "eyes" to share the beauty in his stead.

Some people called Muhammad Ali a "big mouth," meaning he talked too much in an offensive or tactless way. But actually, he had a "loud" mouth with a "big" heart! Ali was fearless on speaking his mind about the truth, but his compassionate nature overshadowed the negative comments. As stated by his family and friends in many documentaries, especially on the Public Broadcasting Stations (PBS), Ali has emptied his pockets and given clothes off his back worth thousands of dollars to the homeless and total strangers on the streets on countless occasions. Moreover, he received the Liberty Medal for his position as an advocate for humanitarian causes, equality, peace, and racial justice throughout the world.

Ali's "loud mouth" became his trademark, so to speak. As part of his "self-promotion" he would often, use humorous name-calling, funny jokes, slogans, and rhyming phrases to describe the situation or to antagonize his boxing opponent. This was all done in good faith for publicity and to leave a lasting impression. The attention practices worked because the crowds loved it! Muhammad Ali was loved by so many, both for his contributions to society and his generous personality. In and out of the ring, he gained the respect of being *the whole package.*

The Greatest Champ

He's beautiful, courageous, and bold.
      Of his victories, a story is told.
With boastful talk and strength of a clamp,
      He won the title of "Heavyweight Champ."
His motto "I float like a butterfly
      And sting like a bee"
Is amazing to watch as he shuffles his feet.
      Muhammad Ali is his name.
Throughout the world, he earned his fame.
      But one unfortunate night, he lost that
Which was so dear to his heart.
      Feeling so assured of himself,
He failed to do his job.
      In a matter of moments, his title was gone.
And from the air of the audience,
      Hurt was shown.
Beaten as he is, but not to stay,
      He is determined to
Recapture his glory another day.
      But if that day of recovery is not obtained,
He needs not go through life
      Bearing a cross of shame.
In the millions of minds, a seal is stamped,
      Saying,
"Muhammad Ali is the Greatest of All Champs!"

Others

A Few Moments with You

I didn't see it coming.
It took us both by surprise.
But just a few moments with you
Were like a lifetime in paradise.

Your warm, affectionate,
And loving ways
Made me forget
Our tender and seasoned age.

Emotions running
Like a rushing stream,
Giggling and playing
Like excited teens.

What a wonderful night,
An unforgettable scene,
Like a script from a movie
Or an impossible dream.

The "elements" all lined up,
Each setting a special tone.
The heavens sent "sparks" and "stars,"
While earth supplied a "perfect song."

What a dance! What a "Tennessee Waltz" chance
To experience the magic that only God could produce.
He created the precise rhythm and time
For an incredible *moment with you*!

Life Is a Rainbow without You

My life is a rainbow
Since you went away.
My feelings reveal the colors
With each passing day.

I cried up a storm
That eventually disappeared.
But it left this rainbow
To remind me that you're not here.

My eyes are always *red*,
Which reflects that I've been crying.
My mind is a total *black*out,
Which shows I'm almost dying.

My days are all *blue*
For fear of never being with you.
My skies are always cloudy and *gray*
Even when it's a sun-shinny day.

Although the storm has blown over,
The forecast is still gloomy and dark.
Scattered showers continue to pop up
In the cracks of my broken heart.

But someday,
I know the rain will cease,

And we both can see clearly again
Because fate will guide you back to me.

Until that magic moment,
When everything will unfold,
I'll be at the end of that rainbow.
I hope to be *your pot of gold!*

The Heart

It's warm.
It loves so sweet.
It weeps
When hurt so deep.

It longs for affection.
It wants to be stress-free
From toxic relationships
That trigger irregular beats.

It desires a gentle touch,
A warm embrace,
Wrapped securely in the arms
Of a waiting "soul mate"

My Clothes Won't Cooperate: Annotation

This poem is especially dedicated to Carolyn "CJ" Jackson. When she heard the statement blurted out, "My clothes won't cooperate," she instantly adopted the slogan. She thought the expression was figuratively hilarious! The lyrics literally evolved from CJ's inspiration and enthusiasm. I am sure this will be her "saying" for life.

Although the clothes conversations are described in a humorous and metaphorical fashion, every woman, at one point in her life, can attest to a similar situation, regardless of the size. However, the proper diet and exercise are the key to "making amends" but first you must *name it and claim it!*

My Clothes Won't Cooperate

Got a date
Running late
In despair
Don't know what to wear.

No time to try
On this and that
When I find things that fit
They just don't match.

And just when I had
It all figured out
The whole rack of clothes
Began to shout!

"If you lose some *weight*,
Maybe we'll *cooperate*!"

Every day
I get ugly sounds
Moans, groans
And nasty frowns

Comments and jokes
That hit below the belt
Only describes
How miserable I felt.

I decided to exercise
To show my regrets
Then the *gym suit*
Cringed in a cold sweat

My sexy *tight jeans*
Began to scream
"If you as much as cough or sneeze,
I will split every seam!"

The sassy *red dress*
Instantly got depressed
For fear of being
Tried on next

The *turtle neck sweater*
Began to choke,
Saying, "Who gains weight
In the throat!"

That low-cut *black dress*
With buttons from bottom to top
Said, "As soon as you take a seat,
They are all going to pop!"

The white *tease blouse*
With the see-through sleeves
Cried, "Don't stick those fat arms through here
And make me bleed!"

My expandable *pencil skirt*
Pleaded, "I'm already hard to zip.
If I stretch any more,
Every thread is going to rip!"

The go-to *leggings*
Joined in with a pout,

Saying, "I, too,
Am all *stretched* out!"

Even the *shoes* weighed in
With a little wisecrack:
"If you squeeze those 'swole up' feet in me,
I will definitely squeeze back!"

"I'll have you reeling and rocking
Like a worn out wagon wheel.
And you'll probably play it off
Like you've broken a heel."

"There will be so much
Misery and pain.
You'll end up
Carrying me in your hand."

One by one
They ranted and raged
And read me my rights
As I stood in a daze

"Enough is enough," they cried!
"How could you do this to us
When you know eventually
We would put up a fuss?"

"It has always been
Clearly understood
That we work together
To make 'each other' look good."

"We used to hug your bottom,
So round and fine.
Men would take a second look
At your cute behind."

"Like the time when this car,
Ran in the ditch,
Because the driver couldn't take his eyes
Off your curvy hips."

"Let's get back to
The way things used to be,
When every garment
Would fit to a T."

"We all agree
That you're beautiful inside and out,
And our only wish
Is to make you proud."

"You don't have to reminisce
On the days of old.
Get your swagger back,
And make us look like brand-new clothes."

"All you have to do
Is lose those *extra pounds*.
We'll be right here waiting,
Just "hanging" around.

P.S.
"Stop telling your friends
How bad we've 'treated' you.
If only they knew
How desperately we've 'needed' you
To show us off
And make those '*haters*' *hate*!
Because that's what we do
When we stand firmly and *cooperate*!"

Appendix A

Note of Thanks

Ms. Shirley,

I was reading the book of Daniel the other day and came across the stories of "The writings on the wall" and "Daniel in the lions pen". I immediately thought about the songs you taught us in Drill Team. I appreciate you so much for teaching us the word of God in a fun, interactive way. You know that someone has truly made an impact when over 20 years later, I can still remember all of the words. I need you to know that you are appreciated, and your labor is not in vain.

With Thanks!

Constance D. Darby

Appendix B

"Clearly Outstanding" Performance Assessment Record

Appendix C

Biblical Reference

The High Cost of Low Living

David and Bathsheba

One evening David got up from his bed and walked around on the roof of the palace. From the roof he saw a woman bathing. *The woman was very beautiful, and David sent someone to find out about her.* The man said, "*She is Bathsheba,* the daughter of Eliam and *the wife of Uriah the Hittite.*" Then *David sent messengers to get her.* She came to him, and *he slept with her.* (Now she was purifying herself from her monthly uncleanness.) Then she went back home. *The woman conceived and sent word to David,* saying, "I am pregnant." *So David sent this word to Joab: "Send me Uriah the Hittite."* And Joab sent him to David.

Then David said to Uriah, "Go down to your house and wash your feet." *So Uriah left the palace,* and a gift from the king was sent after him. *But Uriah slept at the entrance to the palace with all his master's servants and did not go down to his house.*

David was told, "*Uriah did not go home.*" So he asked Uriah, "Haven't you just come from a military campaign? Why didn't you go home?"

Uriah said to David, "The ark and Israel and Judah are staying in tents, and my commander Joab and my lord's men are camped in the open country. *How could I go to my house to eat and drink and make love to my wife?* As surely as you live, *I will not do such a thing!"*

Then David said to him, "Stay here one more day, and tomorrow I will send you back." So Uriah remained in Jerusalem that day and the next. At David's invitation, he ate and drank with him, and *David made him drunk. But in the evening Uriah went out to sleep on his mat among his master's servants; he did not go home.*

In the morning *David wrote a letter to Joab and sent it with Uriah. In it he wrote, "Put Uriah out in front where the fighting is fiercest. Then withdraw from him so he will be struck down and die."*

When the men of the city came out and fought against Joab, some of the men in David's army fell; moreover, Uriah the Hittite died…

When Uriah's wife heard that her husband was dead, she mourned for him. After the time of mourning was over, David had her brought to his house, and *she became his wife and bore him a son. But the thing David had done displeased the* LORD. (2 Sam. 11:2–6, 8–15, 17, 26 NIV; emphasis added)

Suggested reading: 2 Samuel 11:1–26

Nathan rebukes David (the child dies)

Then David said to Nathan, "I have sinned against the LORD.*"* Nathan replied, "The LORD has taken away your sin. You are not going to die. But because by doing this you have shown utter contempt for the LORD, *the son born to you will die.*"

After Nathan had gone home, *the LORD struck the child that Uriah's wife had borne to David*, and he became ill. *David pleaded with God for the child.* He fasted and spent the nights lying in sackcloth on the ground. On the seventh day the child died…(2 Sam. 12:13–16, 18 NIV; emphasis added)

Suggested reading: 2 Samuel 12:1–23

Jezebel killed (thrown from a window)

Then Jehu went to Jezreel. *When Jezebel heard about it, she put on eye makeup, arranged her hair and looked out of a window.* As Jehu entered the gate, she asked, "Have you come in peace, you Zimri, you murderer of your master?"

He looked up at the window and called out, "Who is on my side? Who?" Two or three eunuchs looked down at him. *"Throw her down!" Jehu said. So they threw her down, and some of her blood spattered the wall and the horses as they trampled her underfoot.*

Jehu went in and ate and drank. "Take care of that cursed woman," he said, *"and bury her,* for she was a king's daughter." *But when they went out to bury her, they found nothing except her skull, her feet and her hands.* They went back and told Jehu, who said, *"This is the word of the LORD that he spoke through his servant Elijah* the Tishbite: *On the plot of ground at Jezreel, dogs will devour Jezebel's flesh. Jezebel's body will be like dung on the ground* in the plot at Jezreel, so that no one will be able to say, 'This is Jezebel.'" (2 Kings 9:30–37 NIV; emphasis added)

Samson and Delilah

Sometime later, *he fell in love with a woman in the Valley of Sorek whose name was Delilah. The rulers of the Philistines went to her and said, "See if you can lure him into showing you the secret of his great strength and how we can overpower him* so we may tie him up and subdue him. *Each one of us will give you eleven hundred shekels of silver." So Delilah said to Samson, "Tell me the secret of your great strength and how you can be tied up and subdued."*

Then she said to him, "How can you say, 'I love you,' when you won't confide in me? This is the third time you have made a fool of me and haven't told me the secret of your great strength. *With such nagging she prodded him day after day until he was sick to death of it. So he told her everything.* "No razor has ever been used on my head," he said, "because *I have been a Nazirite dedicated to God from my mother's womb. If my head were shaved, my strength would leave me,* and *I would become as weak as any other man."*

When Delilah saw that he had told her everything, she sent word to the rulers of the Philistines, "Come back once more; he has told me everything." So the rulers of the Philistines returned with the silver in their hands. *After putting him to sleep on her lap,* she called for someone to shave off the seven braids of his hair, and so began to subdue him, *And his strength left him. Then she called, "Samson, the Philistines are upon you!" He awoke from his sleep and thought, "I'll go out as before and shake myself free." But he did not know that the LORD had left him. Then the Philistines seized him, gouged out his eyes* and took him down to Gaza. *Binding him with bronze shackles, they set him to grinding grain in the prison.* (Judg. 16:4–6, 15–21 NIV; emphasis added)

Suggested reading: Judges 16:1–31

Jesus sentenced to be crucified

Finally Pilate handed him over to them to be crucified. So the soldiers took charge of Jesus. *Carrying his own cross*, he went out to the place of the Skull (which in Aramaic is called *Golgotha*). There they crucified him, and with him two others—one on each side and Jesus in the middle. (John 19:16–18 NIV; emphasis added)

The Crucifixion of Jesus

Two other men, both criminals, were also led out with him to be executed. *When they came to the place called the Skull, they crucified him there, along with the criminals*—one on his right, the other on his left. *Jesus said, "Father, forgive them, for they do not know what they are doing."* (Luke 23:32–34 NIV; emphasis added)

Note: Calvary means the same as *Golgotha*. According to the New Testament, Jesus was crucified at a spot outside Jerusalem called Golgotha, which in Aramaic means *"place of the skull."* The Latin word for skull is *calvaria*, and in English, many Christians refer to the site of the crucifixion as *Calvary.*

God Doesn't Have to Use You and Me

Star

After Jesus was born in Bethlehem in Judea, during the time of King Herod, Magi from the east came to Jerusalem and asked, "Where is the one who has been born king of the Jews? We saw his *star* when it rose and have come to worship him." (Matt. 2:1–2 NIV; emphasis added)

Suggested reading: Matthew 2:1–12

Muddy waters

So Naaman arrived with his horses and chariots and stood at the door of Elisha's home. Elisha sent a messenger out to tell him to *go and wash in the Jordan River seven times and he would be healed of every trace of his leprosy!* But Naaman was angry and stalked away...

Aren't the Abana River and Pharpar River of Damascus better than all the rivers of Israel put together? If it's rivers I need, I'll wash at home and get rid of my leprosy." So he went away in a rage. But his officers tried to reason with him and said, "If the prophet had told you to do some great thing, wouldn't you have done it? So you should certainly obey him when he says simply to go and wash and be cured!" *So Naaman went down to the Jordan River and dipped himself seven times, as the prophet had told him to. And his flesh became as healthy as a little child's, and he was healed.* (2 Kings 5:9–14 TLB; emphasis added)

Suggested reading: 2 Kings 5:1–15

Water turned to wine

On the third day a wedding took place at Cana in Galilee. Jesus' mother was there, and *Jesus and his disciples had also been invited to the wedding. When the wine was gone, Jesus' mother said to him, "They have no more wine."*

His mother said to the servants, "Do whatever he tells you." Nearby stood six stone water jars, the kind used by the Jews for ceremonial washing, each holding from twenty to thirty gallons.

Jesus said to the servants, "Fill the jars with water"; so they filled them to the brim.

Then he told them, "Now draw some out and take it to the master of the banquet."

They did so, *and the master of the banquet tasted the water that had been turned into wine.* He did not realize where it had come from, though the servants who had drawn the water knew. *Then he called the bridegroom aside and said, "Everyone brings out the choice wine first and then the cheaper wine after the guests have had too much to drink; but you have saved the best till now."* (John 2:1–3, 5–10 NIV; emphasis added)

Suggested reading: John 2:1–11

Clay dirt

As he went along, *he saw a man blind from birth.* His disciples asked him, "Rabbi, who sinned, this man or his parents, that he was born blind?" "Neither this man nor his parents sinned," said Jesus, "but this happened so that the works of God might be displayed in him.

After saying this, *he spit on the ground, made some mud with the saliva, and put it on the man's eyes.* "Go," he told him, "wash in the Pool of Siloam." So *the man went and washed, and came home seeing.* (John 9:1–3, 6–7 NIV; emphasis added)

Suggested reading: John 9:1–11)

Dew

Then Gideon said to God, "If you are truly going to use me to rescue Israel as you promised, prove it to me in this way. I will put a wool fleece on the threshing floor tonight. *If the fleece is wet with dew* in the morning *but the ground is dry,* then *I will know that you are going to help me* rescue Israel *as you promised.*" And that is just what happened. When Gideon got up early the next morning, he squeezed the fleece and wrung out a whole bowlful of water. (Judg. 6:36–38 NLT; emphasis added)

Suggested reading: Judges 6:1–40)

Sun

But Paul, threatening with every breath and eager to destroy every Christian, went to the High Priest in Jerusalem. He requested a letter addressed to synagogues in Damascus, requiring their cooperation in the persecution of any believers he found there, both men and women, so that he could bring them in chains to Jerusalem.

As he was nearing Damascus on this mission, *suddenly a brilliant light from heaven spotted down upon him! He fell to the ground and heard a voice saying to him, "Paul! Paul! Why are you persecuting me?"* "Who is speaking, sir?" Paul asked.

And the voice replied, "I am Jesus, the one you are persecuting! Now get up and go into the city and await my further instructions."

The men with Paul stood speechless with surprise, for they heard the sound of someone's voice but saw no one! *As Paul picked himself up off the ground, he found that he was blind.* He had to be led into Damascus and was there three days, blind, going without food and water all that time. (Acts 9:1–9 TLB; emphasis added)

Suggested reading: Acts 9:1–22

Clouds (by day) and fire (by night)

After leaving Sukkoth, they camped at Etham on the edge of the desert. *By day*, the Lord went ahead of them in *a pillar of cloud to guide them* on their way and *by night* in *a pillar of fire* to give them light, so that they could travel by day or night. Neither the pillar of cloud by day nor the pillar of fire by night left its place in front of the people. (Exod. 13:20–22 NIV; emphasis added)

Shade (from a tree)
Jonah's anger at the Lord's compassion

Then *the Lord God provided a leafy plant* and made it grow up *over Jonah to give shade for his head to ease his discomfort*, and Jonah was very happy about the plant. (Jonah 4:6 NIV; emphasis added)

Suggested reading: Jonah 4:1–11

Shade tree taken away

> But at dawn the next day, *God provided a worm, which chewed the plant so that it withered.* When the sun rose, *God provided a scorching east wind, and the sun blazed on Jonah's head* so that he grew faint. He wanted to die, and said, "It would be better for me to die than to live." (Jonah 4:7 NIV; emphasis added)

Suggested reading: Jonah 4:1–11

Wind (to dry a path)

> Then Moses stretched out his hand over the sea, and *all that night the LORD drove the sea back with a strong east wind and turned it into dry land. The waters were divided, and the Israelites went through the sea on dry ground, with a wall of water on their right and on their left.* (Exod. 14:21–22 NIV; emphasis added)

Sea (The Red Sea)

> The *water* flowed back and *covered the chariots and horsemen*—the *entire army* of Pharaoh *that had followed the Israelites into the sea. Not one of them survived.*
>
> But the Israelites went through the sea on dry ground, with a wall of water on their right and on their left. *That day the LORD saved Israel from the hands of the Egyptians,* and Israel saw the Egyptians lying dead on the shore. (Exod. 14:28–30 NIV)

Suggested reading: Exodus 14:21–31

It's a "King" Thing

The woman at the well
Jesus talks with a Samaritan woman at Jacob's well

Now Jesus learned that the Pharisees had heard that he was gaining and baptizing more disciples than John—although in fact it was not Jesus who baptized, but his disciples. So he left Judea and went back once more to Galilee.

Now he had to go through Samaria. So he came to a town in Samaria called Sychar, near the plot of ground Jacob had given to his son Joseph. *Jacob's well was there, and Jesus, tired as he was from the journey, sat down by the well. It was about noon.*

When *a Samaritan woman came to draw water, Jesus said to her, "Will you give me a drink?"* (His disciples had gone into the town to buy food.) *The Samaritan woman said to him, "You are a Jew and I am a Samaritan woman. How can you ask me for a drink?"* (For *Jews do not associate with Samaritans.*)

Jesus answered her, "If you knew the gift of God and who it is that asks you for a drink, you would have asked him and he would have given you living water." "Sir," the woman said, *"you have nothing to draw with and the well is deep. Where can you get this living water? Are you greater than our father Jacob,* who gave us the well and drank from it himself, as did also his sons and his live-stock?" *Jesus answered,* "Everyone who drinks this water will be thirsty again, *but whoever drinks the water I give them will never thirst.* Indeed, *the water I give them will become in them a spring of water welling up to eternal life."* The woman said to him, "*Sir, give me this water* so that I won't get thirsty and have to keep coming here to draw water."

He told her, "Go, call your husband and come back." "*I have no husband,*" she replied.

Jesus said to her, "You are right when you say you have no husband. *The fact is, you have had five husbands, and the man you now have is not your husband.* What you have just said is quite true."

"*Sir,*" the woman said, "*I can see that you are a prophet.* Our ancestors worshiped on this mountain, but *you Jews claim that the place where we must worship is in Jerusalem.*"

"*Woman,*" Jesus replied, "believe me, *a time is coming when you will worship the Father neither on this mountain nor in Jerusalem.* You Samaritans worship what you do not know; we worship what we do know, for salvation is from the Jews. *Yet a time* is coming and *has now come when the true worshipers will worship the Father in the Spirit and in truth, for they are the kind of worshipers the Father seeks. God is spirit, and his worshipers must worship in the Spirit and in truth.*"

The woman said, "I know that Messiah" (called Christ) "*is coming. When he comes, he will explain everything to us.*"

Then Jesus declared, "I, the one speaking to you—I am he."

The disciples rejoin Jesus

Just then his disciples returned and were surprised to find him talking with a woman. But no one asked, "What do you want?" or "Why are you talking with her?"

Then, leaving her water jar, the woman went back to the town and said to the people, "Come, see a man who told me everything I ever did. Could this be the Messiah?" They came out of the town and made their way toward him.

Meanwhile *his disciples urged him, "Rabbi, eat something."* But he said to them, *"I have food to eat that you know nothing about."* Then his disciples said to each other, "Could someone have brought him food?" *"My food," said Jesus, "is to do the will of him who sent me and to finish his work.* Don't you have a saying, 'It's still four months until harvest'? I tell you, open your eyes and look at the fields! They are ripe for harvest. Even now the one who reaps draws a wage and harvests a crop for eternal life, so that the sower and the reaper may be glad together. Thus the saying 'One sows and another reaps' is true. I sent you to reap what you have not worked for. Others have done the hard work, and you have reaped the benefits of their labor."

Many Samaritans believe

Many of the Samaritans from that town believed in him because of the woman's testimony, *"He told me everything I ever did."* So when the Samaritans came to him, they urged him to stay with them, and he stayed two days. *And because of his words many more became believers.* They said to the woman, *"We no longer believe just because of what you said; now we have heard for ourselves,* and *we know that this man really is the Savior of the world."* (John 4:1–42 NIV; emphasis added)

A woman caught committing adultery

But Jesus went to the Mount of Olives.

Now early in the morning He came again into the temple, and all the people came to Him; and He sat down and taught them.

Then *the scribes and Pharisees brought to Him a woman caught in adultery.* And *when they had set her in the midst, they said to Him, "Teacher, this woman was caught in adultery, in the very act.* Now *Moses, in the law, commanded us that such should be stoned.* But *what do You say?"* This they said, testing Him, that they might have *something* of which to accuse Him. *But Jesus stooped down and wrote on the ground with His finger, as though He did not hear.*

So when they continued asking Him, He raised Himself up and said to them, *"He who is without sin among you, let him throw a stone at her first."*

And *again He stooped down and wrote on the ground.* Then *those who heard it, being convicted by their conscience, went out one by one,* beginning with the oldest *even* to the last.

And *Jesus was left alone, and the woman standing in the midst.* When Jesus had raised Himself up and saw no one but the woman, *He said to her, "Woman, where are those accusers of yours? Has no one condemned you?"*

She said, "No one, Lord." And *Jesus said to her, "Neither do I condemn you; go and sin no more."* (John 8:1–11 NKJV; emphasis added)

Martin Luther King Jr. was an American Christian minister and activist who became the most visible spokesperson and *leader in the Civil Rights Movement* from 1955 until his assassination in 1968.

God Has Done Great Things...
Thus, He Has Done Great Things for Me

Rainbow (God's covenant with Noah)

> And God said, "This is the sign of the covenant I
> am making between me and you and every living
> creature with you, a covenant for all generations
> to come: *I have set my rainbow in the clouds, and it
> will be the sign of the covenant between me and the
> earth. Whenever I bring clouds over the earth and
> the rainbow appears in the clouds, I will remem-
> ber my covenant between me and you and all living
> creatures of every kind.* Never again will the waters
> become a flood to destroy all life. (Gen. 9:12–15
> NIV; emphasis added)

Moses led the Israelites out of Egypt

> And now *the cry of the Israelites has reached me,*
> and *I have seen the way the Egyptians are oppressing
> them. So now, go. I am sending you to Pharaoh to
> bring my people the*
>   *Israelites out of Egypt."* But Moses said to
> God, "Who am I that I should go to Pharaoh
> and bring the Israelites out of Egypt?" *And God
> said, "I will be with you..."* (Exod. 3:9–12 NIV;
> emphasis added)

Satan: as a roaring lion

> Be alert and of sober mind. *Your enemy, the devil,
> prowls around like a roaring lion looking for some-
> one to devour.* Resist him, standing firm in the
> faith. (Pet. 5:8–9 NIV; emphasis added)

Satan: to sift you like wheat

> "Simon, Simon, *Satan has asked to sift all of you as wheat.* But I have prayed for you, Simon that your faith may not fail. And when you have turned back, strengthen your brothers." (Luke 22:31–32 NIV; emphasis added)

Satan: ruler of darkness

> Finally, my brethren, be strong in the Lord and in the power of His might. Put on the whole armor of God, that you may be able to stand against the wiles of the devil. *For we do not wrestle against flesh and blood, but against principalities, against powers, against the rulers of the darkness of this age, against spiritual hosts of wickedness in the heavenly places.* (Eph. 6:10–12 NKJV)

The Writing on the Wall

The writing on the wall

> *King Belshazzar gave a great banquet* for a thousand of his nobles and drank wine with them. While Belshazzar was drinking his wine, he gave orders to bring in the gold and silver goblets that Nebuchadnezzar his father had taken from the temple in Jerusalem, so that the king and his nobles, his wives and his concubines might drink from them. *So they brought in the gold goblets that had been taken from the temple of God in Jerusalem, and the king and his nobles, his wives and his concubines drank from them. As they drank the wine, they praised the gods of gold and silver, of bronze, iron, wood and stone.*

Suddenly the fingers of a human hand appeared and wrote on the plaster of the wall, near the lampstand in the royal palace. The king watched the hand as it wrote. His face turned pale and *he was so frightened that his legs became weak and his knees were knocking.*

The king summoned the enchanters, astrologers and diviners. Then he said to these wise men of Babylon, "Whoever reads this writing and tells me what it means will be clothed in purple and have a gold chain placed around his neck, and he will be made the third highest ruler in the kingdom."

Then all the king's wise men came in, but they could not read the writing or tell the king what it meant. So King Belshazzar became even more terrified and his face grew more pale. His nobles were baffled.

The queen, hearing the voices of the king and his nobles, came into the banquet hall. "May the king live forever!" she said. *"Don't be alarmed! Don't look so pale! There is a man in your kingdom who has the spirit of the holy gods in him.* In the time of your father *he was found to have insight and intelligence and wisdom like that of the gods.* Your father, *King Nebuchadnezzar, appointed him chief of the magicians, enchanters, astrologers and diviners.* He did this because *Daniel*, whom the king called Belshazzar, *was found to have a keen mind and knowledge and understanding, and also the ability to interpret dreams, explain riddles and solve difficult problems. Call for Daniel, and he will tell you what the writing means."*

So Daniel was brought before the king, and the king said to him, "Are you Daniel, one of the exiles my father the king brought from Judah? I have heard that the spirit of the gods is in you and that you have insight, intelligence and outstanding wisdom. The wise men and enchanters were brought before me to read this writing and tell me what it means, but they could not explain it. Now I have heard that you are able to give interpretations and to solve difficult problems. If you can read this writing and tell me what it means, you will be clothed in purple and have a gold chain placed around your neck, and you will be made the third highest ruler in the kingdom."

Then Daniel answered the king, "You may keep your gifts for yourself and give your rewards to someone else. Nevertheless, *I will read the writing for the king and tell him what it means.*

"Your Majesty, *the Most High God gave your father Nebuchadnezzar sovereignty and greatness and glory and splendor. Because of the high position he gave him, all the nations and peoples of every language dreaded and feared him. Those the king wanted to put to death, he put to death;* those he wanted to spare, he spared; those he wanted to promote, he promoted; and those he wanted to humble, he humbled. *But when his heart became arrogant and hardened with pride, he was deposed from his royal throne and stripped of his glory. He was driven away from people and given the mind of an animal;* he lived with the wild donkeys and *ate grass like the ox;* and his body was drenched with the dew of heaven, *until he acknowledged* that *the Most High God* is sovereign over all kingdoms on earth and sets over them anyone he wishes.

"*But you, Belshazzar, his son, have not humbled yourself, though you knew all this. Instead, you have set yourself up against the Lord of heaven. You had the goblets from his temple brought to you, and you and your nobles, your wives and your concubines drank wine from them.* You praised the gods of silver and gold, *of bronze, iron, wood and stone, which cannot see or hear or understand. But you did not honor the God who holds in his hand your life and all your ways. Therefore he sent the hand that wrote the inscription.*

"This is the inscription that was written:

MENE, MENE, TEKEL, PARSIN
"Here is what these words mean:
Mene: *God has numbered the days of your reign* and *brought it to an end.*
Tekel: You *have been weighed* on the scales *and found wanting.*
Peres: *Your kingdom is divided* and *given to* the *Medes* and *Persians."*

Then at Belshazzar's command, Daniel was clothed in purple, a gold chain was placed around his neck, and he was proclaimed the third highest ruler in the kingdom.

That very night Belshazzar, king of the Babylonians, was slain, and *Darius the Mede took over* the kingdom, at the age of sixty-two. (Dan. 5 NIV; emphasis added)

Daniel in the Lion's Den

It pleased Darius to appoint 120 satraps to rule throughout the kingdom, with three administrators over them, *one of whom was Daniel.* The satraps were made accountable to them so that the king might not suffer loss. *Now Daniel so distinguished* himself *among the administrators and the satraps by his exceptional qualities* that *the king planned to set him over the whole kingdom. At this, the administrators and the satraps tried to find grounds for charges against Daniel in his conduct of government affairs,* but *they were unable to do so. They could find no corruption in him,* because *he was trustworthy* and *neither corrupt nor negligent. Finally these men said, "We will never find any basis for charges against this man Daniel unless it has something to do with the law of his God."*

So these administrators and satraps went as a group to the king and said: "May King Darius live forever! *The royal administrators, prefects, satraps, advisers and governors have all agreed that the king should issue an edict and enforce the decree that anyone who prays to any god or human being during the next thirty days, except to you.*

Your Majesty, shall be thrown into the lions' den. Now, Your Majesty, issue the decree and put it in writing so that it cannot be altered—in accordance with the law of the Medes and Persians, which cannot be repealed." So King Darius put the decree in writing.

Now when Daniel learned that the decree had been published, he went home to his upstairs room where the windows opened toward Jerusalem. Three times a day he got down on his knees and prayed, giving thanks to his God, just as he had done before. *Then these men went as a group and found Daniel praying* and asking God for help. *So they went to the king and spoke to him about his royal decree:* "Did you not publish a decree that during the next thirty days anyone who prays to any god or human being except to you, Your Majesty, would be thrown into the lions' den?"

The king answered, "The decree stands— in accordance with the law of the Medes and Persians, *which cannot be repealed."*

THE GOSPEL WITH A TWIST AND MORE...

Then they said to the king, "Daniel, who is one of the exiles from Judah, pays no attention to you, Your Majesty, or to the decree you put in writing. He still prays three times a day." When the king heard this, he was greatly distressed; he was determined to rescue Daniel and made every effort until sundown to save him.

Then the men went as a group to King Darius and said to him, "Remember, Your Majesty, that according to the law of the Medes and Persians no decree or edict that the king issues can be changed."

So the king gave the order, and they brought Daniel and threw him into the lions' den. The king said to Daniel, "May your God, whom you serve continually, rescue you!"

A stone was brought and placed over the mouth of the den, and the king sealed it with his own signet ring and with the rings of his nobles, so that Daniel's situation might not be changed. Then the king returned to his palace and spent the night without eating and without any entertainment being brought to him. And he could not sleep.

At the first light of dawn, the king got up and hurried to the lions' den. When he came near the den, he called to Daniel in an anguished voice, "Daniel, servant of the living God, has your God, whom you serve continually, been able to rescue you from the lions?"

Daniel answered, "May the king live forever! *My God sent his angel, and* he shut the mouths of the lions. They have not hurt me, *because* I was found innocent in his sight. Nor have I ever done any wrong before you, Your Majesty."

The king was overjoyed and gave orders to lift Daniel out of the den. And when Daniel was lifted *from the den, no wound was found on him, because he had trusted in his God.*

At the king's command, the men who had falsely accused Daniel were brought in and thrown into the lions' den, along with their wives and children. And before they reached the floor of the den, the lions overpowered them and crushed all their bones.

Then King Darius wrote to all the nations and peoples of every language in all the earth:

"May you prosper greatly!

"I issue a decree that in every part of my kingdom people must fear and reverence the God of Daniel. "For *he is the living God* and endures forever; his kingdom will not be destroyed, his dominion will never end. He rescues and he saves; he performs signs and wonders in the heavens and on the earth. He has rescued Daniel from the power of the lions."

So Daniel prospered during the reign of Darius and the reign of Cyrus the Persian. (Dan. 6 NIV; emphasis added)

The Mighty Fire

Moses and the burning bush

There the angel of the LORD appeared to him *in flames of fire from within a bush.* Moses saw that *though the bush was on fire it did not burn up.* So Moses thought, *"I will go over and see this strange sight—why the bush does not burn up."* (Exod. 3:2–3 NIV; emphasis added)

Suggested reading: Exodus 3:1–21

Three Hebrew boys in the fiery furnace: Shadrach, Meshach, and Abednego

Nebuchadnezzar spoke, saying to them, *"Is it true, Shadrach, Meshach, and Abed-Nego, that you do not serve my gods or worship the gold image which I have set up?*

Then Nebuchadnezzar was full of fury, and the expression on his face changed toward Shadrach, Meshach, and Abed-Nego. *He spoke and commanded that they heat the furnace seven times more than it was usually heated.* And *he commanded certain mighty men of valor who were in his army to bind* Shadrach, Meshach, and Abed-Nego, *and cast them into the burning fiery furnace.*

Therefore, *because the king's command was urgent,* and *the furnace exceedingly hot, the flame of the fire killed those men* who took up *Shadrach, Meshach, and Abed-Nego.* And these three men, Shadrach, Meshach, and Abed-Nego, fell down bound into the midst of the burning fiery furnace.

Then King Nebuchadnezzar was astonished; and he rose in haste *and* spoke, *saying* to his counselors, *"Did we not cast three men bound into the midst of the fire?"*

They answered and said to the king, "True, O king."

"Look!" he answered, *"I see four men loose, walking in the midst of the fire; and they are not hurt,* and *the form of the fourth is like the Son of God."* (Dan. 3:14, 19–25 NKJV; emphasis added)

Suggested reading: Chapter 3:1–30

I Don't Want Rocks Crying Out for Me

Rocks crying out!

> As he rode along, the crowds spread out their garments on the road ahead of him. When he reached the place where the road started down the Mount of Olives, *all of his followers began to shout and sing as they walked along, praising God for all the wonderful miracles they had seen.*
>
> But *some of the Pharisees* among the crowd said, *"Teacher, rebuke your followers for saying things like that!" He replied, "If they kept quiet, the stones along the road would burst into cheers!"* (Luke 19:36–37, 39–40 NLT; emphasis added)

Rooster

> *Peter declared,* "Even if everyone else deserts you, I will never desert you."
>
> *Jesus replied,* "I tell you the truth, Peter— *this very night, before the rooster crows, you will deny three times that you even know me."* (Matt. 26:33–34 NLT; emphasis added)

Dry bones

> *"I will put flesh and muscles on you and cover you with skin. I will put breath into you, and you will come to life. Then you will know that I am the* LORD.*"*
>
> So I spoke this message, just as he told me. Suddenly *as I spoke, there was a rattling noise all across the valley. The bones of each body came together and attached themselves as complete skeletons.* So I spoke the message as he commanded

me, and breath came into their bodies. *They all came to life and stood up on their feet*—a great army. (Ezek. 37:6, 7, 10 NLT; emphasis added)

Suggested reading: Ezekiel 37:1–10

Whale

Now *the LORD provided a huge fish to swallow Jonah*, and *Jonah was in the belly of the fish three days and three nights.*

And *the LORD commanded the fish*, and *it vomited Jonah onto dry land.* (Jonah 1:17, 2:10 NIV; emphasis added)

Ram

Abraham looked up and *there in a thicket he saw a ram* caught by its horns. *He went over and took the ram and sacrificed it as a burnt offering instead of his son.* (Gen. 22:13 NIV; emphasis added)

Suggested Reading: Genesis 22:1–14

Rod

"What do you have there in your hand?" the Lord asked him. And he replied, "*A shepherd's rod.*" "Throw it down on the ground," the Lord told him. So he threw it down—*and it became a serpent*, and Moses ran from it! Then the Lord told him, "Grab it by the tail!" He did, and it became a *rod* in his hand again! *"Do that and they will believe you!"* the Lord told him. "*Then they will realize that* Jehovah, the *God* of their ancestors

Abraham, Isaac, and Jacob, *has really appeared to you.*

And *be sure to take your rod along so that you can perform the miracles I have shown you."* (Exod. 4:2–5, 17 TLB; emphasis added)

Suggested Reading: Exodus 3:7–21, 4:1–17

Locust

And the locusts covered the land of Egypt from bor-der to border; it was the worst locust plague in all Egyptian history; and there will never again be another like it. For the locusts covered the face of the earth and blotted out the sun so that the land was darkened; and they ate every bit of vegetation the hail had left; there remained not one green thing—not a tree, not a plant throughout all the land of Egypt. (Exod. 10:14–15 TLB; emphasis added)

Suggested Reading: Exodus 10:1–19)

Frogs

Then the Lord said to Moses, "Go in again to Pharaoh and tell him, 'Jehovah says, "Let my people go and worship me. If you refuse, I will send vast hordes of frogs across your land from one border to the other. The Nile River will swarm with them, and they will come out into your houses, even into your bedrooms and right into your beds! Every home in Egypt will be filled with them. They will fill your ovens and your kneading bowls; you and your people will be immersed in them!""" Then the Lord said to Moses, "Instruct Aaron to point the rod toward all the rivers, streams, and pools of Egypt, so that there will be frogs in every corner of the land." Aaron did, and frogs covered the nation. (Exod. 8:1–6 TLB; emphasis added)

Suggested reading: Exodus 8:1–15

Dove

After forty days Noah opened a window he had made in the ark…

Then he sent out a dove to see if the water had receded from the surface of the ground.

But the dove could find nowhere to perch because there was water over all the surface of the earth; so it returned to Noah in the ark. He reached out his hand and took the dove and brought it back to himself in the ark. *He waited seven more days and again sent out the dove from the ark. When the dove returned to him in the evening, there in its beak was a freshly plucked olive leaf! Then Noah knew that the water had receded* from the earth. (Gen. 8:6, 8–11 NIV; emphasis added)

Manna

In the desert, *the whole community grumbled against Moses and Aaron.* The Israelites said to them, "If only we had died by the LORD's hand in Egypt! There we sat around pots of meat and ate all the food we wanted, but *you have brought us out into this desert to starve* this entire assembly to death." Then the LORD said to Moses, *"I will rain down bread from heaven* for you.

The people of Israel *called the bread manna.* It was white like coriander seed and tasted like wafers made with honey. Moses said, "*This is what the* LORD *has commanded*: '*Take an omer of manna and keep it for the generations to come, so they can see the bread I gave you to eat in the wilderness when I brought you out of Egypt.*'"

The Israelites ate manna forty years, until they came to a land that was settled; they ate manna until they reached the border of Canaan. (Exod. 16:2–4, 31–32, 35 NIV; emphasis added)

Suggested reading: Exodus 16:1–36

The Magical Three (3)

Three Wise Men

Now when Jesus was born in Bethlehem of Judaea in the days of Herod the king, behold, *there came wise men from the east to Jerusalem, Saying, Where is he that is born King of the Jews?* for we have seen his star in the east, and are come to worship him. (Matt. 2:1–2 KJV; emphasis added)

Suggested reading: Matthew 2:1–12

Three temptations of Jesus

Then was Jesus led up of the Spirit into the wilderness to be tempted of the devil.

And when the tempter came to him, he said, If thou be the Son of God, command that these stones be made bread.

Then the devil taketh him up into the holy city, and setteth him on a pinnacle of the temple, And saith unto him, If thou be the Son of God, cast thyself down:

Again, the devil taketh him up into an exceeding high mountain, and sheweth him all the kingdoms of the world, and the glory of them; *And saith unto him, All these things will I give thee, if thou wilt fall down and worship me.* (Matt. 4:1, 3, 5–6, 8–9 KJV; emphasis added)

Suggested reading: Matthew 4:1–11

Three nights in the belly of a whale

Now the LORD provided a huge fish to swallow Jonah, and *Jonah was in the belly of the fish three days and three nights.* (Jonah 1:17 NIV; emphasis added)

Suggested reading: Matthew 1:1–17

Three of Job's Friends

When Job's three friends, Eliphaz the Temanite, Bildad the Shuhite and Zophar the Naamathite, heard about all the troubles that had come upon him, they set out from their homes and met together by agreement to go and sympathize with him and comfort him. When they saw him from a distance, they could hardly recognize him; they began to weep aloud, and they tore their robes and sprinkled dust on their heads. (Job 2:11–12 NIV; emphasis added)

Suggested reading: Job 2:1–13

Three boys refused to bow

Shadrach, Meshach and *Abednego replied to* him, "*King Nebuchadnezzar,* we do not need to defend ourselves before you in this matter. If we are thrown into the blazing furnace, the *God we serve is able to deliver us* from it, and he will deliver us from Your Majesty's hand. *But even if he does not, we want you to know, Your Majesty* that *we will not serve your gods or worship the image of gold you have set up."* (Dan. 3:16–18 NIV)

Suggested reading: Daniel 3:1–30

Three Times Denied

Jesus answered, "I tell you, Peter, before the rooster crows today, you will deny three times that you know me.

    About an hour later another asserted, *"Certainly this fellow was with him, for he is a Galilean." Peter replied, "Man, I don't know what you're talking about!" Just as he was speaking, the rooster crowed. The Lord turned and looked straight at Peter.* Then Peter remembered the word the Lord had spoken to him: "Before the rooster crows today, you will disown me three times." And he went outside and wept bitterly. (Luke 22:34, 59–62 NIV)

Suggested reading: Luke 22:34, 59–62

Three days later, Jesus Rose

For what I received I passed on to you as of first importance: that *Christ died for our sins according to the Scriptures, that he was buried, that he was raised on the third day according to the Scriptures.* (1 Cor. 15:3–4 NIV; emphasis added)

Suggested reading: 1 Corinthians 15:3–8

The Master Has Done Great Things

Wet cloth

> Then Gideon said to God, "If you are truly going to use me to rescue Israel as you promised, prove it to me in this way. I will put a wool fleece on the threshing floor tonight. *If the fleece is wet with dew* in the morning *but the ground is dry*, then *I will know that you are going to help me* rescue Israel *as you promised." And that is just what happened.* When Gideon got up early the next morning, he squeezed the fleece and wrung out a whole bowlful of water. (Judg. 6:36–38 NLT; emphasis added)

> Suggested reading: Judges 6:36–40

The sun, parked in the sky

> On the day the LORD gave the Amorites over to Israel, Joshua said to the LORD in the presence of Israel: "Sun, stand still over Gibeon, and you, moon, over the Valley of Aijalon."
> *So the sun stood still and the moon stopped, till the nation avenged itself on its enemies,* as it is written in the Book of Jashar. *The sun stopped in the middle of the sky and delayed going down about a full day.* There has never been a day like it before or since, a day when the LORD listened to a human being. Surely the LORD was fighting for Israel! (Josh. 10:12–14 NIV; emphasis added)

The valley of dry bones

> Then he said to me, "Prophesy to these bones and say to them, '*Dry bones*, hear the word of the LORD!

So I spoke this message, just as he told me. *Suddenly as I spoke, there was a rattling noise all across the valley. The bones of each body came together and attached themselves* as complete skeletons.

So I prophesied as he commanded me, and breath entered them; they came to life and stood up on their feet—a vast army. (Ezek. 37:4, 7, 10 NIV; emphasis added)

Suggested reading: Ezekiel 37:1–10

Revelation of John

I, John, your brother and companion in the suffering and kingdom and patient endurance that are ours in Jesus, *was on the island of Patmos because of the word of God and the testimony of Jesus. On the Lord's Day I was in the Spirit,* and *I heard behind me a loud voice like a trumpet, which said: "Write on a scroll what you see and send it to the seven churches: to Ephesus, Smyrna, Pergamum, Thyatira, Sardis, Philadelphia* and *Laodicea."*

"Write, therefore, what you have seen, what is now and what will take place later. The mystery of the seven stars that you saw in my right hand and of the seven golden lampstands is this: *The seven stars are the angels of the seven churches,* and *the seven lampstands are the seven churches.* (Rev. 1:9–11, 19–20 NIV; emphasis added)

Suggested reading: Revelation 1:1–11
Concerning the churches: Revelation 2:1–29 and 3:1–22

The DeGreprobate State(s)

But mark this: *There will be terrible times* in the last days. *People will be lovers of themselves, lovers of money, boastful, proud, abusive, disobedient to their parents, ungrateful, unholy, without love, unforgiving, slanderous, without self-control, brutal, not lovers of the good, treacherous, rash, conceited, lovers of pleasure rather than lovers of God*—having a form of godliness but denying its power. Have nothing to do with such people.

T*hey* are the kind who worm their way into homes and *gain control over gullible women, who are loaded down with sins* and are *swayed by all kinds of evil desires*, always learning *but never able to come to a knowledge of the truth.* Just as Jannes and Jambres opposed Moses, so also *these teachers oppose the truth. They are men of depraved minds*, who, as far as the faith is concerned, are *rejected.* But they will not get very far because, as in the case of those men, their folly will be clear to everyone.

A Final Charge to Timothy

You, however, know all about my teaching, my way of life, my purpose, faith, patience, love, endurance, persecutions, sufferings—what kinds of things happened to me in

Antioch, Iconium and Lystra, the persecutions I endured. *Yet the Lord rescued me from all of them.* In fact, everyone who wants to live a godly life in Christ Jesus will be persecuted, while *evildoers and impostors will go from bad to worse, deceiving and being deceived.* But as for you, continue in what you have learned and have become convinced of, because you know those from whom you learned it, and *how from infancy you have known the Holy Scriptures, which are able to make you wise for salvation through faith in Christ Jesus.* All Scripture is God-breathed and is useful for teaching, rebuking, correcting and training in righteousness, so that the servant of God may be thoroughly equipped for every good work. (2 Tim. 3 NIV; emphasis added)

One Wish

An angel gave me *one wish*,
With the world, I wanted to share.
"Riches" would cloud the view to heaven,
Hardly anyone would make it there.

Since the love of money is the root of all evil,
There would evolve many schemes and plots.
The "haves" would surely find a way
To swindle and steal from the "have-nots."

Remarkably, I found the perfect solution
For *all* to enjoy an abundant life!
My *one wish* is that "everyone"
Could be like Jesus Christ!

About the Author

Currently residing in Houston, Texas, Shirley Collins was born and raised in Lake Providence, Louisiana (East Carroll Parish). The youngest of nine siblings (five girls and four boys), she was the first in her family to attend college and receive a degree. Her father, a World War I veteran, worked for the East Carroll Parish Highway Department, and her mother was a housewife who also worked part-time at the school cafeteria. Her family includes five generations that number well over three hundred (9 siblings, 48 grandchildren, 100 great grandchildren, 128 great-great-grandchildren, and 30 great-great-great-grandchildren).

Shirley's modest early life experiences served as the catalyst for the emergence of her imaginative and creative spirit, as well as her steadfast faith in the Lord and His Word. As she continues to stand on God's promises, Shirley is an operative member of the church, devoting her time and service to several departments and volunteering whenever is needed. She plans to broaden her writing scope to include another passion, a collection of children's books.

To satisfy her exuberant spirit and the love of student involvement, Shirley considers herself only as "semiretired," while she remains active in the education arena as a high school substitute teacher.

CPSIA information can be obtained
at www.ICGtesting.com
Printed in the USA
JSHW021206310323
39660JS00006B/61